Young Justice

PETER DAVID
KARL KESEL
GEOFF JOHNS
BEN RAAB
JAY FAERBER
D. CURTIS JOHNSON
CHUCK DIXON
DWAYNE MCDUFFIE
BRIAN K. VAUGHAN
TODD DEZAGO
SCOTT BEATTY
JIM ALEXANDER
writers

YOUNG JUSTICE

LARY STUCKER
KEITH CHAMPAGNE
ROB HAYNES
MARK LIPKA
JAIME MENDOZA
CHRIS IVY
JASON BAUMGARTNER
NORM RAPMUND
WALDEN WONG
WAYNE FAUCHER
JUAN VLASCO
RICH FABER
RODNEY RAMOS
SCOTT KOBLISH
WADE VON GRAWBADGER
CULLY HAMNER
inkers

TODD NAUCK
CARLO BARBERI
SUNNY LEE
TOM GRUMMETT
ROB HAYNES
CARY NORD
ANGEL UNZUETA
DREW JOHNSON
SCOTT KOLINS
MICHAEL AVON OEMING
MIKE MILLER
NORM BREYFOGLE
CULLY HAMNER
pencillers

KEN LOPEZ
COMICRAFT
BILL OAKLEY
DAVE LANPHEAR
SEAN KONOT
CHRIS ELIOPOULOS
CLEM ROBINS
ALBERT T. DE GUZMAN
letterers

MIKE WIERINGO &
TERRY AUSTIN

TOM GRUMMETT &
KARL KESEL

TODD NAUCK &
LARY STUCKER
original covers

JASON WRIGHT
TOM MCCRAW
PAT GARRAHY
BUZZ SETZER
DAVID SELF
NOELLE GIDDINGS
MOOSE BAUMANN
JOE ROSAS
RICK TAYLOR
colorists

YOUNG JUSTICE: SINS OF YOUTH

Originally published in single magazine form as YOUNG JUSTICE: SINS OF YOUTH 1-2, SUPERBOY 74, SINS OF YOUTH SECRET FILES 1, SINS OF YOUTH: JLA, JR. 1, SINS OF YOUTH: AQUABOY/LAGOON MAN 1, SINS OF YOUTH: BATBOY AND ROBIN 1, SINS OF YOUTH: KID FLASH/IMPULSE 1, SINS OF YOUTH: STARWOMAN AND THE JSA (JUNIOR SOCIETY) 1, SINS OF YOUTH: SUPERMAN, JR./SUPERBOY, SR. 1, SINS OF YOUTH: WONDER GIRLS 1, SINS OF YOUTH: THE SECRET/DEADBOY 1.

DC Comics, 1700 Broadway, New York, NY 10019

A division of Warner Bros. -
A Time Warner Entertainment Company

Printed in Canada. First Printing.

ISBN: 1-56389-748-2

Cover illustration by Mike Wieringo and Terry Austin

Cover color by Richard and Tanya Horie

Publication design by Murphy Fogelnest

AT A DESERTED RESORT HOTEL IN THE CATSKILL MOUNTAINS, THE YOUTHFUL HEROES KNOWN COLLECTIVELY AS "YOUNG JUSTICE" HAVE TAKEN REFUGE.
UNDER FIRE FROM BOTH ENEMIES AND ALLIES, THEIR CAVE HQ RUBBLE, THEY WANT ONLY A RESPITE AT THIS POINT.
IT'S NICE TO WANT THINGS.
LOOK AT ALL THE ROOMS! WE CAN HAVE OUR PICK OF--
WONDER GIRL! THE BALLROOM, NOW!
B-182
THAT WAS ROBIN! OH, HERA, NOW WHAT?
IMPULSE! BALLROOM! NOW!
WHAT, ARE WE HAVING AN EMERGENCY DANCE OR SOMETHING?
SECRET! BALLROOM!
WONDER GIRL SAID, "NOW!"
YEEP!

YEARS AGO, THEY SERVED AS SIDEKICKS, AS YOUNG HEROES.
NOW THEY SERVE AS THE VOICE OF A NATION THAT DOESN'T TRUST ITS YOUNG PEOPLE TO KNOW THE DIFFERENCE BETWEEN RIGHT AND WRONG.
THEY HAVE BEEN OPERATING MOSTLY FROM BEHIND THE SCENES, BUT NOW--AFTER DECADES OF OBSCURITY--THEY HAVE RECLAIMED THE LIMELIGHT.
THEY ARE...
OLD JUSTICE
...AND THEY'RE NOT JUST THE SAME OLD THING.

Justice for All

PETER DAVID writer · TODD NAUCK penciller · LARY STUCKER inker · JASON WRIGHT colorist · KEN LOPEZ letterer · MAUREEN McTIGUE associate editor · EDDIE BERGANZA editor

THEIR OPPOSITION, YOUNG JUSTICE NATURALLY.

OKAY, KIDS... IT'S *OVER*. THERE'RE FOLKS IN WASHINGTON WHO WANT TO *TALK* TO YOU. NO NEED TO MAKE THIS INTO ANY MORE OF A MEDIA FEEDING FRENZY THAN IT'S *ALREADY* BEEN.

YOU'RE IN NO POSITION TO KNOW, OR JUDGE, WHAT WE DO OR DO NOT "NEED."

WHAT HE SAID! IT'S NOT OVER UNTIL WE SAY IT'S OVER!

C'MON, GUYS! LET'S GET 'EM!

GUYS?

FOR THE LUVVA...! WHAT'RE YOU STANDING THERE FOR?

ROBIN... DO WE HAVE TO...?

I KNOW... I SEE THE PROBLEM...

WHAT PROBLEM? 'CAUSE THEY'RE OLD? ARE YOU KIDDIN'? MAX IS OLDER'N ALL OF 'EM PUT TOGETHER, HE COULD PROBABLY TAKE US ON NO SWEAT.

EVEN SO...

EVEN SO WHAT? WHAT'S GOING ON?

I DID PRISON TIME, BOY, 'CAUSE NO ONE--EVEN MY OLD PARTNER, HOURMAN--BEAT ANY SENSE INTO ME. WELL, SPARE THE ROD, SPOIL THE CHILD.
SURE, FINE, OLD MAN, WHATEVER YOU S--
--AAAAAY!
GUESS WHAT, PUNK? EVERYTHING OLD IS NEW AGAIN!
AWWWWW NO YOU DON'T!
CHOOSE YOUR TARGETS! ATTACK AT WILL! BUT USE CAUTION, AND TRY NOT TO--
"--HURT US,"? YES, YOUR CONCERN IS TOUCHING!
BUT WE CYCLONE TWINS WERE ADVENTURING BACK WHEN YOUR DADDY WAS IN SHORT PANTS, KIDDO, SO DON'T WORRY ABOUT US!

DON'T WORRY, ROB! I'LL GET'CHA OUT!
LEFT ON YOUR OWN, YES, YOU LIKELY WOULD.
BUT MARBLES FILLED WITH CLOUDS OF GAS... WELL, THAT'S A LITTLE GIMMICK THAT'LL MAKE IT A BIT MORE OF A CHALLENGE.
OKAY, THAT'S IT!
OOOOF!
WELL WELL WELL.
IS THAT IT, DYNAMITE MAN?! IS THAT ALL YA GOT?
C'MON! BRING IT!
C'MON!!
"BRING IT," PUNK? HERE IT IS!
UNNNNH!
They were just trying to be NICE! They felt sorry for you!
GOTTA LITTLE GIZMO READY FER YOU, SPOOKY.
And THIS is what you do! How dare you! How--
HUH?
LIKE YOOS KIDS SEZ, "SUX T'BE YOO!"

YOU'RE DISPERSING THE GAS VERY NICELY, IMPULSE.
BUT YOUR BRAIN'S STILL A BIT FOGGY.. SLOWING YOU DOWN FOR MY LITTLE GIMMICK SPRING TO HOGTIE YOU.
VIBRATE ALL YOU WANT. WON'T WORK. THINK OF IT AS A GIANT SHOCK ABSORBER.
BELIEVE IT OR NOT, MERRY, YOU DON'T HOLD THE PATENT ON GIMMICKS... ALL APPEARANCES TO THE CONTRARY NOTWITHSTANDING.
OOOO! WAS THAT AN AGE JOKE, BIRDBOY?
I'VE RESEARCHED YOU "CYCLONE TWINS" SINCE OLD JUSTICE CAME ON THE SCENE.
YOU GO BY "DINKY" AND "SISTY," SO I WOULDN'T MAKE FUN OF MY NAME IF I WERE YOU.
PERHAPS WE ALL HAVE A LOT TO LEARN THEN, EH, ROBIN?
ZWAM
UNHHH!
YOU'RE PROB'LY RIGHT, DANNY BOY.
SO HERE'S YOUR CHANCE TO SEE THE LIGHT.

DAN! MOVE!
UNHHH!!!
IT'S... IT'S WEARING OFF! THE PILL... IT'S WEARING OFF! GET THIS THING OFF ME!
BLAST IT OFF HIM, DAN! HURRY!
CAN'T! HAVEN'T RECHARGED YET!
GET IT OFF! SECONDS ONLY SECONDS BEFORE--!
OH, CALM DOWN! DID YOU WHINE THIS MUCH WHEN YOU WERE WITH THE MINUTEMEN?
THERE! YOU'RE FREE, SECRET! NOW LET'S CLEAN HOUSE!
THANKS, Wonder Girl!
That... that LIGHT! BLINDING! Is it a UFO?! The face of GOD?!

NOPE! IT'S ACE ATCHINSON! CDTV! ON THE SCENE AT THE SECRET HEADQUARTERS OF YOUNG JUSTICE, AS WE WITNESS STILL MORE OF THE RELENTLESS PERSECUTION THAT HAS BEEN INFLICTING THIS YOUNG TEAM OF LATE!
DAN THE DYNAMITE! YOU'VE TOLD ANYONE WITH A MICROPHONE AND CAMERA THAT THESE KIDS ARE DANGEROUS! WOULD YOU MIND TELLING OUR VIEWERSHIP... WHO THREW THE FIRST PUNCH HERE?
WELL... THAT'S NOT THE POINT...
HE DID!
THAT guy right there!
HIS NAME'S THORNDYKE! HE DECKED SUPERBOY!
UHHH... THAT OLD GUY DID?
OBVIOUSLY ABSURD! THORNY, "DECK" SUPERBOY! LOOK AT HIM! THE NOTION'S ABSUR--
DAN!!
PROTECTIN' OUR OWN IZ ONE T'ING, BUT BOTTOM LINE, BAD GUYS LIE...
AND HEROES TELL TH'TROOT! THE KIDS'RE RIGHT! THORNY TOOK A PILL THAT JAZZED 'IM UP, AND YEAH, A FEW MINUTES AGO, HE WUZ DANG'ROUS!
BUT IT WORE OFF, AND HE WOULD'A DIED, 'CEPT SUPER CHICK THERE SAVED 'IM.
THAT'S WONDER CHICK...UH, WONDER GIRL.

WE JUST CAME TO TALK, BUT THINGS GOT OUT OF HAND...
BUT AS SENIORS, ISN'T IT YOUR RESPONSIBILITY NOT TO LET THINGS GET OUT OF HAND?
YES. YOU'RE ABSOLUTELY RIGHT. THAT'S WHY WE WANTED TO HAVE THE KIDS SURRENDER TO US SO THAT WE CAN PEACEFULLY--
PEACEFULLY RAILROAD US! BETWEEN THE PRESS AND THE POLITICIANS, NO ONE WANTS TO HEAR OUR SIDE OF IT! EMPOWERED TEENAGERS SPOOK EVERYBODY!
THAT'S SIMPLY NOT TRUE!
TO SOME DEGREE, IT IS.
PART OF GROWING UP IS LEARNING HOW TO SURVIVE IN THE WORLD. NATURALLY, WE ALL WANT TO KNOW THAT OUR PARENTS LOVE US AND WANT TO WATCH OUT FOR US.
AND YES, THERE HAVE BEEN TRAGEDIES THAT ARE RELATED TO TEENS.
BUT THE RESULT HAS BEEN PARANOIA. TEENS HAVE REPLACED POSTAL WORKERS AS AMERICA'S CLICHÉD POWDER KEGS.
EITHER WE'RE "DANGEROUS," OR ELSE SO HELPLESS THAT WE NEED SCHOOLS TURNED INTO ARMED CAMPS TO "PROTECT" US.

AND FREEDOM OF EXPRESSION BECOMES COMPLETELY STIFLED, LYRICS TO MUSIC BECOME SUPPRESSED, AND EVERYTHING GETS BLAMED ON MARILYN MANSON OR SOMETHING.
IT'S LIKE... EVERYONE LIKES TO LOOK AT THINGS AS BLACK OR WHITE, EXCEPT THERE ARE HUES OF GREY AND IT'S ALL SOMEWHERE IN THE MIDDLE.
WELL, THAT'S WHAT TEENS ARE-- IN THE MIDDLE OF BEING KIDS AND BEING ADULTS. EXCEPT WE'RE NOT AS CUTE AS KIDS, AND ADULTS CONDESCEND TO US. TREAT US LIKE KIDS WHILE EXPECTING US TO BE ADULTS. NO, "ACT" LIKE ADULTS. THAT'S WHAT WE'RE TOLD. LIKE IT'S ALL A GAME.
AND IT'S LIKE ADULTS ARE SAYING, "WE HAVE TO HELP TEENAGERS SO THEY DON'T NAPALM A NURSERY SCHOOL OR SOMETHING."
WELL, Y'KNOW WHAT? WE'RE NOT THE ENEMY, AND WE'RE NOT BABIES TO BE PROTECTED!
MAYBE, LIKE, WHAT WE NEED IS LESS PROTECTING AND MORE BEING LISTENED TO.

CONTESSA...YOU DO NOT SEEM TO UNDERSTAND! FORTRESS CADMUS IS FALLEN! AMANDA SPENCE JUST ESCAPED! SHE--!
I ALREADY KNOW IT AND HAVE PREPARED FOR IT.
YOU EXPECTED THIS?!
I EXPECT NOTHING, GARFIELD...BUT ANTICIPATE EVERYTHING.
I HAVE ALREADY ACTIVATED AN ALTERNATE PLAN. I'M WATCHING AN ELEMENT OF IT NOW, AND THE OTHER SHOULD BE ALONG SHORTLY.
IN THE MEANTIME, PUT OUR SPECIALIZED GROUND TROOPS ON STANDBY AND HAVE THEM AWAIT MY ORDERS. I BELIEVE THAT MATTERS MAY BE COMING TO A BOIL... AND I HAVE JUST THE PERSON IN MIND TO STIR THE POT.
WELL, WELL, WELL. I WAS SPEAKING TO A HOLOGRAM OF ONE OF MY PEOPLE ABOUT YOU.
...KLARION THE WITCH BOY.
I WANT YOU TO ADD A "BUM BUM BUM."
ADD... WHAT?
MY NAME NEEDS MORE DRAMA TO IT. SO I DESIRE TO BE...
...KLARION... BUM BUM BUM... THE WITCH BOY!
I WILL NOT ADD A MUSICAL STING TO YOUR NAME.
AS YOU WISH. BEST OF LUCK WITH YOUR PLANS.
WAIT! COME BACK, KLARION...
ALL RIGHT. NOW WE CAN TALK.
:SIGH:... BUM BUM BUM... THE WITCH BOY.

ROBIN WANTS ME TO TALK ABOUT EVERYTHING THAT'S *HAPPENED*. PRESENT OUR *CASE*. GUYS, I CAN'T KEEP THIS *UP*. I CAN'T *DO* THIS.

ARE YOU *KIDDIN'!?* YOU'RE DOIN' *GREAT!*

EVEN *I* ALMOST BELIEVE YOU!

OH, *THANKS*, BART.

THEY'RE *RIGHT*. YOU'RE HANDLING THIS *PERFECTLY*.

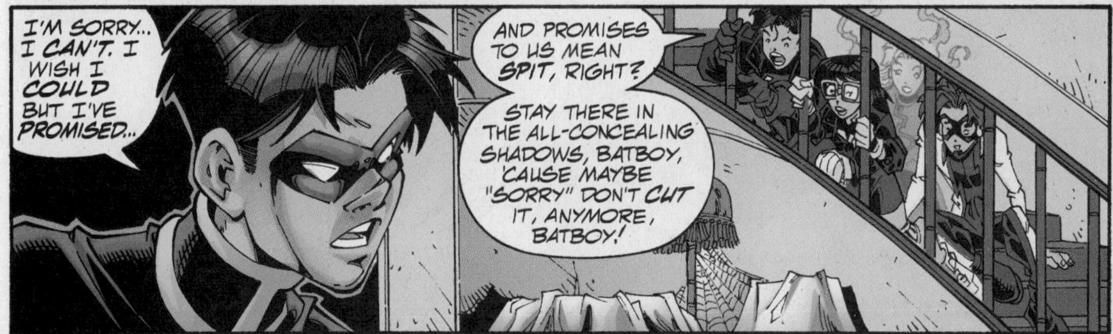

OKAY, KIDDIES, LET'S MAKE **MAGIC**.

COULD YOU LOSE THE **CIGARETTE**, PLEASE, MISS? SUPER-VILLAINS ARE BAD **ENOUGH**. I DON'T NEED TO DEAL WITH SECOND-HAND SMOKE.

FIGURES.

WHERE YOU WANNA **SET UP?**

OW!!

UHM... THE ALL-CONCEALING SHADOWS JUST SAID "OW."

HEY, BILLY... MARY... WHAT ARE YOU WATCH--
SHHH!!
FIRST OFF, IN RESPONSE TO THE STORY THAT WAS PUT FORWARD ON THE SENATE FLOOR...YES. ONE OF OUR MEMBERS--AN ARCHER--DID TRACK DOWN A MAN, RICHARD PULILO.
PULILO MURDERED AN INNOCENT WOMAN. IN THE HEAT OF BATTLE, THE ARCHER ALMOST KILLED HIM... BUT ANOTHER MEMBER PREVENTED IT. NEED I POINT OUT THAT, IF THE POLICE HAD CAUGHT UP WITH HIM, A SHOOTOUT WOULD HAVE LEFT HIM, AND POSSIBLY POLICEMEN, DEAD.
THE FACT THAT PULLIO IS STILL ALIVE TO COMPLAIN IS A TESTAMENT TO OUR GROUP, NOT A CONDEMNATION. THE ARCHER, MEANTIME, HAS RETIRED FROM ACTIVE DUTY, HOLDING HERSELF TO AN ETHICAL STANDARD MOST "CIVILIANS" WOULDN'T.
WE'RE "IRRESPONSIBLE"? C'MON. WE WATCH OUT FOR OWN, AND WE ACKNOWLEDGE WHEN WE SHOULD NOT BE PURSUING CAREERS AS SUPER-HEROES.
AS FOR THE UNFORTUNATE BUSINESS WITH MT. RUSHMORE...
ONE OF OUR MEMBERS, WHO'S BEEN OUR SECRET, WAS KIDNAPPED BY A GOVERNMENT ORGANIZATION CALLED THE ALL PURPOSE ESPIONAGE SQUAD. SHE COMMITTED NO CRIME, BUT HER RIGHTS WERE BEING TRAMPLED ON.
HOW TO DRAW COMICS THE DC WAY
SO WE RESCUED HER. UNFORTUNATELY, "A.P.E.S." HQ IS HIDDEN INSIDE OF MT. RUSHMORE. WHEN A.P.E.S. ATTACKED US, WE DEFENDED OURSELVES, AND PART OF THE MEMORIAL BECAME DAMAGED. OBVIOUSLY WE'RE SORRY ABOUT THAT...

...BUT Y'KNOW WHAT? IT'S MADE OF UNFEELING STONE. SECRET, HERE...SHE'S A REAL PERSON. SEE? FLESH AND BLOOD AND... AND...
SMOKE.
UH...YEAH. THAT TOO.
AND SHE WAS, LIKE, SCARED AND ALONE PRAYING THAT HER FRIENDS WOULD COME AND SAVE HER FROM PREDATORY ADULTS WHO WERE PREYING ON HER.
WOW. POOR KID.
YEAH.
AW, FRED, MARY, C'MON! FELONIOUS ASSAULT AND DESTRUCTION OF A NATIONAL MONUMENT...
...AND THEY TRY AND MAKE IT SOME SORT OF ADULT VS. TEENS THING? WHO'S GONNA FALL FOR SOMETHING LIKE THAT?
SERVOTRON
YOUR WHOLE GENERATION BITES!
CARE TO HANDLE THIS?
ALL YOURS.
THANKS LOADS, AL.
FIGURES. THE GOVERNMENT AND ITS PET HOUNDS HARASSING ANYONE WHO TALKS BACK. WHEN WILL PEOPLE REALIZE THAT TOUGH CHOICES ARE GONNA HAVE TO BE MADE?
THE NEXT THING WE KNOW, A GROUP CALLING ITSELF THE POINT MEN INVADED OUR H.Q.
AGAIN THERE WAS PROPERTY DAMAGE, AND THE JLA CAME DOWN ON US LIKE A TON OF BRICKS. THAT'S WHAT HURT US THE MOST, Y'KNOW?

FOR HER AGE, SHE PUTS FORWARD THEIR CASE RATHER ELOQUENTLY, WOULDN'T YOU SAY?
I DETECT A BIT OF BIAS, DIANA.
AS DO I, BUT THAT DOES NOT NEGATE THE ACCURACY OF HER COMMENT.
IF ANYONE IS GOING TO BE BIASED, TORNADO, IT'S LIKELY TO BE YOU.
AND IF ANYONE IS GOING TO BE INTERESTED IN TRUTH AND JUSTICE, SUPERMAN... IT IS LIKELY TO BE YOU.
TOUCHÉ, BIG GUY.
AND THANKS TO THIS WHOLE MEDIA FEEDING FRENZY, WE'RE MADE TO FEEL LIKE CRIMINALS. WE--
M90271
S42173
K31100
IMPULSE! ENOUGH WITH THE PICTURES!
I HAVEN'T READ OR HEARD ONE STORY THAT CUT US ANY SLACK.
IT'S LIKE PEOPLE CAN'T WAIT TO TEAR US DOWN. LIKE THEY'RE SAYING ANYONE WHO'S YOUNG AND SUPER-POWERED CAN'T BE TRUSTED. AND SOMETHING SHOULD BE DONE ABOUT IT.
SLAP

LIKE WHAT?
LIKE A... UH... UHM...
...A...A RALLY! THE JUSTICE FOR ALL RALLY!
WE DON'T WANT OUR STORY BEING TRIED IN THE MEDIA WITHOUT US. SINCE WASHINGTON D.C. IS THE CENTER OF THE CONTROVERSY, WE'LL MEET TOMORROW, 6 P.M., ON THE GREAT LAWN.
FURTHERMORE, WE INVITE ANY ADULT HEROES WHO ARE INTERESTED TO ATTEND.
I KNOW THAT OLD JUSTICE WILL CERTAINLY BE THERE... TO MAKE SURE THAT NO INJUSTICES OCCUR.
IT'LL BE GREAT TO HAVE YOU.
HEY, MAX! I'M ON TV!
IN THE NAME OF GOD, SWITCH TO "THE PRICE IS RIGHT," WOULD YOU, DOC?
--CAN'T BUH-LEEVE YOU DID THAT! A GOOD THING WE'RE OFF THE AIR!!
UH... ACTUALLY... I THINK WE'RE STILL--
AND ANOTHER THING--!

WE'RE GOING, RIGHT? THERE'S NO QUESTION ABOUT THIS.
AH, YEAH, WE'RE GOING.
HELLO? A RALLY FOR HEROES TO COME TOGETHER IN ONE PLACE... IT COULD BE A SET UP. A TRAP. LET'S GIVE SOME SERIOUS THOUGHT TO--
AHEM.
--SETTING THE VCR TO TAPE ANY SHOWS WE WANT TO SEE TOMORROW SINCE, YEAH, WE'RE ALL GOING TO BE IN WASHINGTON.
IT'S GOING TO BE A ZOO, AND THE WHOLE THING SOUNDS SUSPICIOUS. COUNT ME OUT.
BILLY, SOMETIMES YOU CAN BE SUCH A... A GROWNUP!
HOW'D I DO?
YOU DID GREAT.
THANKS.

CONFUSION, KLARION. CHAOS.
THOSE THINGS WHICH ARE THE ANTITHESIS OF WHAT THESE SO-CALLED HEROES STAND FOR. THAT IS WHAT WE'RE TRYING TO INTRODUCE.
I CERTAINLY HAVE SOME FAMILIARITY WITH CRAFT; BUT WHY TARGET THE YOUNG HEROES, SUCH AS THE JUNIOR JLA?
THE COSTUMED ADVENTURERS CAN HANDLE DIRECT ASSAULTS AGAINST WHICH THEY CAN USE THEIR POWERS. BUT SUBTLETY, CRAFT... THESE THEY HAVE NO DEFENSE AGAINST.
BECAUSE THEY ARE EASIER TARGETS. "TODAY'S YOUNG PEOPLE ARE UNIFORMLY BOORISH, RUDE TO THEIR ELDERS, MEAN-SPIRITED AND DANGEROUS." DO YOU KNOW WHO SAID THAT?
GEORGE W. BUSH?
A GREEK PHILOSOPHER, ACTUALLY, OVER TWO THOUSAND YEARS AGO.
THE CONFUSION IS GREATER THAN EVER TODAY. ADULTS USED TO BE AFRAID OF DARK STRANGERS WHO WOULD HURT THEIR YOUNG.
NOW THE DARK STRANGER MIGHT BE SITTING IN ALGEBRA CLASS WITH A SHORT FUSE AND A GUN..
PARENTS WHO HAPPILY LEFT THEIR BRATS WITH STRANGERS, WHILE THEY PURSUED THE ALMIGHTY DOLLAR, ARE NOW DESPERATELY TRYING TO RECONNECT WITH THOSE SAME CHILDREN.
COMPASSION? OR CONCERN THAT THEIR OWN CHILDREN MIGHT BECOME THE NEXT SLAUGHTERERS OF INNOCENTS?

AAAHH. AND IF RELATIVELY NORMAL TEENS CAN STRIKE TERROR INTO THE HEARTS OF ADULTS...
... HOW MUCH EASIER IT IS TO HAVE METAHUMAN TEENS STRIKE EVEN GREATER FEAR INTO THE HEARTS OF ADULTS...
PRECISELY.

I SEE. SO THE NOTION IS TO GET AT THE OLDER HEROES... BY STRIKING AT THE YOUNGER.
YES. YOUTH GROUPS ARE THE WEAK LINK IN THE CHAIN OF HEROING.

IF ONE POLICEMAN SNAPS UNDER PRESSURE AND TRIES TO SHOOT A MURDERER, NO ONE WOULD SUGGEST GETTING RID OF ALL POLICEMEN.
BUT ONE YOUNG HERO BECOMES UNSTRUNG, AND WE CAN TURN IT INTO A MEDIA FEEDING FRENZY. CALL FOR A BAN ON ALL OF THEM.
I NEED YOU TO ADD TO THE CONFUSION, MY DEAR. PEOPLE FEAR WHAT THEY CAN'T CONTROL... SUCH AS YOUTH. THE MORE YOUTHFUL HEROES, THE MORE FEAR. AND THE FEWER ADULTS TO OVERSEE THE SITUATION... THE BETTER.

I LOVE IT! YES! YES! THIS IS DEFINITELY A GLORIOUS CHALLENGE FOR KLARION...

...BUM BUM BUM... THE WITCH BOY!

THE ONLY THING I WISH TO SAY AT THIS TIME--
--IS THAT, CONSIDERING WONDER GIRL HERSELF ADMITS THAT THE JUSTICE LEAGUE HAS "COME DOWN ON THEM LIKE A TON OF BRICKS," THAT SHOULD TELL YOU SOMETHING.
THAT'S IT, THAT'S ALL. THANK YOU.
NEPTUNE. I THOUGHT WE'D HAVE A CHAT.
AQUAMAN! HOW DID YOU GET IN MY PRIVATE OFFICE?
SWAM IN THROUGH THE TOILET. MY POWERS HAVE CHANGED. I CAN NOW GO ANYWHERE THERE'S WATER.
THAT'S...THAT'S AMAZING! HOW HANDY TO--
I WAS KIDDING, NEPTUNE.
I KNEW THAT.
YOU'VE SEEN THE DANGER OF BELIEVING EVERYTHING YOU HEAR?
MEANING?
CONTRARY TO WONDER GIRL'S...WONDERFUL SPEECH, YOUNG PEOPLE ARE THE ONES WHO SEE THE WORLD IN TERMS OF BLACK AND WHITE.
IT'S EVEN MORE LIKELY THAT THEY'LL FEEL THAT WAY WHEN THEY'RE YOUNG SUPER-HEROES, LIVING IN A WORLD OF "GOOD GUYS" AND "BAD GUYS" WITH NOTHING IN BETWEEN.
BATMAN NOTWITH-STANDING.
URBAN LEGEND. DOESN'T COUNT.
RIIIIGHT.
THE POINT IS, NEPTUNE...DESPITE YJ'S BELIEF, WE ARE NOT ALLIED AGAINST THEM.
WE WERE JUST RETHINKING THE NEED OF ONE-TO-ONE SUPERVISION, BUT WE HAVE NO INTENTION OF DISBANDING THE TEAM. AND HEARING HOW THEY WERE HARASSED...

THIS "SECRET" INDIVIDUAL... MY SOURCES SAY SHE WAS TAKEN INTO CUSTODY BECAUSE OF THE NATIONAL SECURITY HAZARD THAT SHE--
HAS SHE COMMITTED A CRIME?
NOT THAT WE KNOW OF, BUT SHE PRESENTS A TREMENDOUS POTENTIAL FOR DANGER...

SO DO WE.
YOU LOOK PARCHED, NEPTUNE. PERHAPS YOU SHOULD WET YOURSELF. OR HAVE YOU ALREADY?

THAT'S THE CONSTITUTION OF THE UNITED STATES. IT SAYS NO ONE CAN BE IMPRISONED WITHOUT DUE PROCESS. THAT INCLUDES "SECRET."
SHE'S A THREAT TO--
NATIONAL SECURITY, YES, I KNOW.
ODDLY, SHE'S BEEN AT LARGE FOR SOME TIME AND THE NATION IS STILL STANDING. AND WE'RE PREPARED TO POINT THAT OUT AT THE JUSTICE FOR ALL RALLY.

YOU'RE NOT ACTUALLY GOING TO BE THERE?
YES. WE ACTUALLY ARE. I KNOW A BIT ABOUT FEEDING FRENZIES, NEPTUNE, AS DO YOU. WE WON'T STAND BY AND SEE YOUNG JUSTICE THROWN TO THE MEDIA SHARKS.
BOTTOM LINE: THEY'RE OUR KIDS, IN SPIRIT IF NOT D.N.A. AND WE PROTECT OUR OWN.

MOVE.

ISN'T IT GREAT THAT WE WERE ALL ABLE TO WORK TOGETHER TO PRODUCE THIS WHOLE BUFFET MEAL?
BETTER THAN TRASHING THE PLACE.
THE THING I STILL DON'T UNDERSTAND IS HOW YOU KNEW WHERE WE WERE. WE HAD BARELY ARRIVED AND YOU WERE HERE. HOW?
YOU'RE GOING TO FIND THIS HARD TO BELIEVE.
TRY ME.
OLD JUSTICE WAS ORIGINALLY CONTACTED BY A WOMAN NAMED AMANDA SPENCE.
SHE SAID SHE BELIEVED IN OUR CAUSE, AND HAD A WAY TO HELP KEEP TABS ON YOU...EVEN LEAD US RIGHT TO YOU, IF THE SITUATION AROSE. NO QUESTIONS ASKED.
THE NEXT THING WE KNEW, WE WERE GETTING TELEPATHIC MESSAGES AS TO WHAT YOU WERE UP TO. I WAS THE MAIN "RECEIVER," MARY AS BACKUP.
THAT'S WHY THERE WAS TV COVERAGE WHEN YOU TRASHED MOUNT RUSHMORE; WE ALERTED THEM, BECAUSE WE WERE ALERTED FIRST.
I DON'T SEE HOW IT'S POSSIBLE! IT'S LIKE SOMEONE WAS READING OUR MINDS!
SINCE ALL OF THIS TRANSPIRED, WE'VE STOPPED HEARING FROM OUR SOURCE. AS IF IT'S BEEN CUT OFF.
SUPERBOY? YOU OKAY?
YEAH...IT'S JUST...KINDA HARD TO BUY, Y'KNOW?
WE'VE NO REASON TO LIE. AND WHY WORRY, ANYWAY?
SOON WE'LL BE IN WASHINGTON AND THIS WILL ALL BE MOOT.

THE TIME IS RAPIDLY APPROACHING. EVERYONE IS WONDERING WHETHER THIS SO-CALLED JUSTICE FOR ALL RALLY WILL ACTUALLY OCCUR, OR WHETHER... WAIT!
I AM GETTING WORD THAT... YES... HEROES ARE APPROACHING THE GREAT LAWN! WE HAVE HEROES, REPEAT, WE HAVE HEROES!
THE JLA HAS BEEN SPOTTED...
...AND THE JSA AS WELL...
AND CAPTAIN MARVEL JUNIOR, AND APPARENTLY HIS DATE...

WHOA-AH! AND THE BIG RED CHEESE HIMSELF HAS JUST SHOWN UP! HIS ASSOCIATES SEEM SURPRISED, FOR SOME REASON.
AND ALSO ON THE WAY ARE THE TEEN TI--
--UHM, THE NEW TI--
--UHM... THE TITAN PEOPLE.
NOT TO MENTION STEEL... SUPERGIRL...
UHM... THE IRON GIANT...
SOME WOMAN WITH A STICK...
AND, APPARENTLY ONE OF THOSE CREATURE COMMANDOS.
ISN'T THIS THE MOST EXCITING THING YOU'VE EVER SEEN? CAN YOU IMAGINE HOW IT MUST BE TO BE ONE OF THEM?
ELIAS
NO. NOT AT ALL.

THOUGHT YOU'D BE UP HERE.
YOU'RE NOT WITH YOUR FRIENDS.
YOU'RE UPSET.
I CAN'T BE. BECAUSE YOU WANT US OUT OF THE LIMELIGHT.
YUP.
I HAVE MY REASONS.
I KNOW. BUT SOMETIMES I THINK THE REASONS AREN'T WHAT YOU THINK THEY ARE.
SOMETHING BIG IS BREWING, MAGIC-WISE. I CAN FEEL IT.
BETTER SCOPE IT OUT... AND SEE IF OL' DEADMAN CAN DO SOMETHING ABOUT IT.
ALL RIGHT, KID... WE'RE HERE. STILL THINK OUR WHOLE GENERATION "BITES"?
WELL... MAYBE NOT ALL OF Y--
LOOK! THERE THEY ARE!
YOUNG JUSTICE

KEEP THOSE CAMERAS BACK!
YOUNG JUSTICE, YOU HAVE ORGANIZED AN ILLEGAL ASSEMBLAGE.
NO PERMITS WERE OBTAINED: YET ANOTHER RECKLESS ACT DUE TO YOUR YOUTH AND INEXPERIENCE.
YOU ARE WANTED FOR QUESTIONING IN SEVERAL SERIOUS MATTERS, AND THIS IS NOT HELPING YOUR CAUSE.
WE'RE HERE BECAUSE WE'RE HAPPY TO ANSWER QUESTIONS. AND ALSO HERE TO LET EVERYONE KNOW--
THAT EVERYTHING THE MEDIA SAID IS TRUE! THEY'RE CRAZY, THE BUNCH OF THEM!
WHAT?!
SUPERBOY, ARE YOU NUTS?!
THEY SHOULD ALL BE LOCKED UP! NOT ONE OF THEM HAS ANY BUSINESS BEING A SUPERHERO! I'LL TURN STATE'S EVIDENCE! ANYTHING! JUST SHUT 'EM DOWN, NOW!
WHAT IN THE--?
OH, THAT'S GONNA BE A GREAT SOUND BITE RIGHT THERE.

OF COURSE!
"OF COURSE" WHAT? SUPERBOY JUST--!
SUPERBOY'S DONE NOTHING. NO WONDER HE HASN'T BEEN ACTING LIKE HIMSELF. WHEN HE HIT THE RED TORNADO... CHALLENGED ME...

...WHEN HE LOOKED SO STARTLED MY LAST DAY AT THE CAVE...WHEN I SAID, "I DON'T KNOW YOU"... HE THOUGHT I REALIZED THAT...

THAT'S NOT SUPERBOY!
HOW CAN YOU BE SURE?

FWOOSH
BECAUSE SUPERBOY TOLD ME THAT HE WAS ONCE CLONED--
WHAT--?
--AND BECAUSE THAT BLINDING STREAK JUST NOW WAS SUPERBOY! WHICH MEANS "OUR" SUPERBOY SINCE ARROWETTE LEFT HAS BEEN--
MAAATCH!!!
UH-OH.

I'M GONNA POUND YOU INTO MATCH STICKS, YOU TWO-BIT--!

OKAY, SETTLE DOWN.
OH, I'LL SETTLE DOWN! RIGHT AFTER I USE MY EVIL TWIN'S HEAD FOR A SOCCER BALL!
THEY'RE TRYING TO TRICK YOU! THEY WANT TO SHUT ME UP, BECAUSE I'M WILLING TO SPEAK THE TRUTH!
J'ONN...? YOU'RE OUR RESIDENT MINDREADER...
HOLD ON.

THIS ONE IS THE IMPOSTOR.
HE'S LYING! THEY'RE IN ON IT, TOO!

ALL RIGHT, THAT'S IT! ARREST THEM ALL!
RIGHT. SURE, I GOT SOME KRYPTONITE IN MY SOCK.

DON'T WORRY ABOUT IT, OFFICERS!
THE POINT MEN AND FRIENDS WILL HANDLE IT!

RIGHT.
SURE.
AS IF WE'D CLUTTER THIS PANEL WITH DIALOGUE. INSTEAD, LET'S CHECK ON KLARION.
NOW... FOR SOME FUN...
THERE! RIGHT THERE!
BRAT'S GOT SOME SORT OF MYSTIC SHIELD UP. CAN'T POSSESS HIM.
BUT THAT'S OKAY. ALWAYS DID PREFER AN ACROBAT'S BODY.
HUH?!
WELL WELL WELL. A TEST CASE.
SUPERB!

ZAP
ZAP
LET'S GO WIDE, AND THRILL TO THE POWER OF KLARION...
...BUM BUM BUM...
...THE WITCH BOY!!!
SEVEN HELLS, I'M GOOD!
YOU ALL LOOK RIDICULOUS.
NOW THAT'S A JUNIOR JUSTICE LEAGUE!!
GREAT HERA!
I'M FASTER!
LIKE HECK!
STOP IT!
FWAM
OOOOFF!
OY! NOW WHAT?!
I DON'T HAVE A GIMMICK TO COVER THIS!
FWIP
MEBBE I DO!

SERPENTEEN BLOCKADE! ROUND THEM UP, WHILE THEY'RE TOO SCARED AND CONFUSED TO FIGHT BACK!
STAY AWAY, Y'MEANIE! I'M A KING AND STUFF!
FAIRPLAY
FAIRPLAY
OH, GO COMMAND A PLATE OF SUSHI, YOU LITTLE SHRIMP.
ARGENT! STARFIRE! TEMPEST! GET THEM OFF THE JLA'S BACKS UNTIL WE CAN GET THIS SORTED OUT!
SKREE
SHORT CUT... I DO BELIEVE THAT'S THE BEST THEY'VE GOT!
IF IT IS, BLOCKADE, IT'S ONLY POLITE TO REROUTE IT BACK TO 'EM!
SKREE
THAT'S IT! TIME TO DO SOME DAMAGE!
SKOW
WHOA! I'M ON YOUR SIDE THERE BOMB BOY!
BOOM

GET BACK HERE! YOU, I'M TURNING INTO A DEAD EMBRYO!
KRA-KOW
YOU JUST PULLED SOMETHING OUT OF YOUR HAT?
YA RATHER I PULLED IT OUTTA MY BUTT? THE HAT WAS A GOIN' AWAY PRESENT FROM...
CHOKE HER.
DOIBY, FIRE THE THING IF IT'S GOING TO BE OF ANY USE!
OH. RIGHT'CHA ARE!
HEY! YJ! GET THE JUSTICE TYKES T'GEDDER AND THEN VAMOOSE!
YOU HOID... UH, HEARD THE MAN! C'MERE!
BUT ME AM HAVING FUN!
YEAH, WELL, ME AM NOT! I SWORE OFF BABY-SITTING AFTER THE LAST DISASTER!
GET BACK IN THERE, WILDBRAT!
AWWW..

WHOEVER THESE SHOCK TROOPS ARE, THEY HAVE SHIELDS ABSORBING MY BLASTS! AND I COULD USE SOME HELP WITH THEIR PULSE CANNONS!
TZZ
CHOOM
TZZ
CHOOM
WE'RE
ON
IT
CYBORG!
GROUNDSWELL! NOW!
HOLY MOLEY!
WHO IS THAT?!
THOUGHT YOU'D NEVER CALL, GRAY LADY!
RRRUMMBLE
JUNIOR!
REGROUP! GET AROUND THAT...THAT WHATEVER IT IS!

WELL, WELL! SEEMS EVEN YOU CAN'T TAKE BEING POUNDED FOREVER, HUH, BLOCKADE!
EEYARRHH!
DIDN'T SEE HIM COMING! THANKS FOR THE ASSIST, CHAOS!
NAME'S "ANARKY!" BUT, HEY, CLOSE ENOUGH, TROIA.
YOU'RE WITH THEM, AREN'T YOU! WITH THE AGENDA... THE ONES WHO IMPRISONED ME... TOOK OVER CADMUS... TURNED IT INTO THE EVIL FACTORY...
YOU--!
YOU'RE FORGETTING SOMETHING, HOTSHOT. I MAY BE MATCH...
BRIGHT BOY. SOMEONE OF NORMAL INTELLIGENCE WOULD HAVE FIGURED IT OUT AGES AGO.
BUT YOU'RE NO MATCH FOR ME!
OOH.
WUMP
NO TIME T'WAIT! THIS THING SHOULD UP-AGE 'EM... I HOPE!
HMM

LOOK, TEEKL! A JUICY LITTLE BIRDIE!
UH OH. WELL... GOTTA FLY.
RRAARRR
ROBIN! I THOUGHT YOU--!
--DIDN'T SHOW? NAH. WOULDN'T MISS IT.
MY SMOKE BOMBS HAVE BOUGHT US SOME COVER! FALL BACK TO--!
We CAN'T! Doiby said to stand here!
DOIBY SAID TO--?
ZWK
AAAKAM
OH NO, YOU DON'T! NO ONE SPOILS MY GOOD TIME!
ZAPPY ZAPPY
IN ONE BLINDING MOMENT, MAGIC AND SUPER-SCIENCE INTERSECT, UNLEASHING ALL MANNER OF POSSIBILITIES IN ONE BLINDING ERUPTION OF LIGHT AND POWER WHICH FLIES IN ALL DIRECTIONS, INCLUDING HEAVENWARD...
ZAA
BOOM
AND WHEN THE SMOKE FINALLY CLEARS...

THE RESULT...
OH, WONDERFUL!
...IS NOT REMOTELY...
CHECK IT! BRING ON THE BABES!
YOU STILL ALL LOOK RIDICULOUS.
...WHAT ANYONE HAD EXPECTED.
AW COME ON! THE ADULTS ARE ALL KIDS OR TEENS... THE TEENS ARE ALL ADULTS...
...AND I'M STILL SIXTEEN?!?
HOW COULD THIS GET WORSE!!

EVERYONE GOES THROUGH GROWING PAINS.
RECENTLY, FOR INSTANCE, MEMBERS OF YOUNG JUSTICE HAVE BEEN ACCUSED OF BEING TOO RECKLESS TO FIGHT FOR TRUTH AND JUSTICE.
SO THE SUPER-COMMUNITY CONVERGED ON WASHINGTON, D.C., TO SHOW SUPPORT FOR THEIR TEENAGE COUNTER-PARTS.
THIS "JUSTICE FOR ALL" RALLY, HOWEVER, TOOK A SURPRISE TURN WHEN EVERYONE UNEXPECTEDLY SWITCHED AGES.
EVERYONE... EXCEPT SUPERBOY!
FIGURES.
THE EVIL FACTORY
GAME, SET & MATCH!
KARL KESEL WRITE-IST
TOM GRUMMETT DRAW-ER
KEITH CHAMPAGNE INK DRAW-ER
BUZZ SETZER USES ALL 64 CRAYONS
COMICRAFT STILL LEARNING JOINED UP WRITING
MIKE MCAVENNIE MAKES US STAY BEHIND AFTER CLASS
JACK KIRBY PRINCIPAL

I MEAN, I'VE ONLY BEEN WAITIN' MY WHOLE LIFE TO BE SUPERMA --
--NNNGH!
KON-EL --!

Oh, THIS IS REALLY GOOD! BETTER THAN THE CONTESSA ASKED FOR! EVEN I'M IMPRESSED! I, KLARION -- BUM, BUM, BUM -- THE WITCH BOY!
AND ALL BECAUSE OF THE MYSTERIOUS MIXTURE OF MY MAGIC...

...AND THAT GEEZER'S WEIRD RAY!
DA KID'S ON DA MONEY, MERRY! DIS WOULDN'TA HAPPENED 'CEPT ON ACCOUNT O' ME!
DOIBY, YOU WERE TRYING TO HELP! WE JUST HAVE TO FIND THE RIGHT GIMMICK TO FIX THINGS...

ALL REPORTERS -- PLEASE STAY BACK. IT'S FOR YOUR OWN SAFETY.
FROM WHO -- THOSE COSTUMES, OR YOU STORM TROOPERS?
CAN ANYONE HEAR WHAT THE HEROES ARE SAYING?
THEY'RE ACTING CRAZY!

YOU HEARD THE LADY, KLARION -- FIX THIS MESS!
BETTER YET -- I'LL MAKE YOU FIX IT!
LIKE YOU HAVE A GHOST OF A CHANCE, DEAD-BOY!
YOU ALWAYS COULD FLY THROUGH THE AIR WITH THE GREATEST OF EASE, BOSTON! LOVED YOUR ACT -- WHEN YOU WERE AN ADULT... AND ALIVE!

IT STILL BRINGS A SMILE TO MY FACE!
COME BACK HERE, YOU HALF-PINT HORROR --!

CALM yourself. we will FIND him.
Huh?! YOU... YOU CAN SEE ME?

WHAT'S WRONG, SUPERBOY?
FEEL RGH! FEEL LIKE I'M... BEIN' TORN APART FROM... THE INSIDE!
BUT... NO PAIN, NO... GAIN, RIGHT? SO MUST BE I'M GONNA... WIN BIG!
YOU'D THINK THE... CONTESSA WOULD... KNOW THAT! CAN'T -- AHG! CAN'T FIGURE WHAT... SHE'S UP TO HERE...
...AND THE GOOD GUYS'VE... ALREADY TAKEN CADMUS BACK FROM... HER AGENDA GOONS!
FORTRESS CADMUS HAS FALLEN?! NO WONDER MY TELEPATHIC LINK WITH THE GENE-GNOME CEASED!
THE AGENDA CREATED ME -- EVEN NAMED ME MATCH SINCE I WAS AT LEAST SUPERBOY'S EQUAL! MY MISSION AND GOAL WAS TO TAKE SUPERBOY'S PLACE...

...BUT I WON'T STAND *IDLE* WHILE THERE MAY STILL BE TIME TO *SAVE* FORTRESS CADMUS!

WE HAVE OUR ORDERS, TOO. *POINT MEN!*

BLANK SLATE -- TAKE US *OUT* OF HERE!

THEY'RE ALL *GETTING AWAY!* WE CAN'T JUST LET THEM *GET AWAY!*

COME ON, *IMPULSE* -- LET'S FIND OUT WHO'S *FASTER* --!

"...AND HIT 'EM HARD!"

ALL RIGHT, PEOPLE -- DON'T OVERDO IT! THEY'RE SCATTERED -- TIME FOR US TO DO THE SAME!
SPLIT UP! MAKE SURE YOU'RE NOT FOLLOWED! REGROUP AT THE JLA CAVE!

HEY, HOW... HOW YOU DOIN', SUPERMAN?
Um... BETTER THAN YOU, I GUESS. FEEL A LITTLE WEAKER THAN NORMAL, MAYBE. NOTHING I CAN'T HANDLE.

GOOD, 'CAUSE... 'CAUSE I GOTTA GET BACK TO CADMUS... STOP MATCH...
...AND HOPE THE PROJECT CAN FIX WHATEVER'S WRONG WITH --
--AHHG!
SUPERBOY!

DON'T WORRY, SUPERMAN-- I'LL HELP HIM!
AND I'D LIKE TO HAVE A FEW WORDS WITH MATCH MYSELF!

-- SAW IT HERE, LIVE! THE YOUNG HEROES AND THEIR MENTORS VICIOUSLY ATTACKING AND OVERWHELMING AN AS-YET UNIDENTIFIED GROUP...
-- UNKNOWN SOLDIERS WHO WERE CLEARLY TRYING TO KEEP THE PEACE!
THERE CAN NOW BE NO DOUBT THAT THESE "JUNIOR JUSTICE LEAGUERS" ARE UNCOOPERATIVE -- AND OUT OF CONTROL!

"YOUNG JUSTICE?" "NO JUSTICE" IS MORE LIKE IT!
PERFECT. MY ORIGINAL PLAN WAS TO DISCREDIT HEROES THROUGH THEIR WEAKEST LINK -- THEIR YOUNG "SIDEKICKS"...
...WHILE SIMULTANEOUSLY USING CADMUS TO CREATE THE AGENDA'S OWN LINE OF ALTERNATIVE HEROES.
THAT PLAN HAS HIT A FEW... SNAGS... BUT I HAD MADE CONTINGENCY PREPARATIONS, AND THEY MOVE FORWARD NICELY...

CONTESSA! THE AGENDA'S HOLD ON CADMUS HAS BEEN BROKEN! ON-SITE LEADER AMANDA SPENCE HAS BEEN CAPTURED!
I STILL HAVE A PLATOON OF CLONE-SOLDIERS BUT NEED REINFORCEMENTS TO RETAKE THE PROJECT! THE POINT MEN --

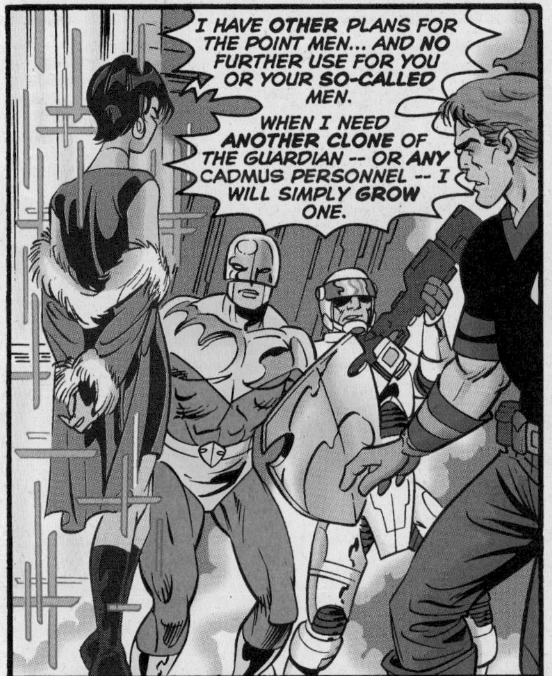
I HAVE OTHER PLANS FOR THE POINT MEN... AND NO FURTHER USE FOR YOU OR YOUR SO-CALLED MEN.
WHEN I NEED ANOTHER CLONE OF THE GUARDIAN -- OR ANY CADMUS PERSONNEL -- I WILL SIMPLY GROW ONE.

SHE... ABANDONED US?
WHAT DO WE DO NOW -- SURRENDER?
NO.

WE'RE CLONES -- BUT WE'RE NOT DISPOSABLE!
WE DON'T GO DOWN WITHOUT A FIGHT!

-- FOUGHT ALL THIS WAY FOR NOTHING **HOWLER**. THE DOOR'S **LOCKED**. CAN'T **OPEN** IT.

WELL NOW, **GORR** -- PERHAPS IF YOU HADN'T TAKEN OUT ITS GUARDS LIKE **TEN-PINS**...

AH RECKON WE COULD USE ONE OF THEM FANCY **CAN OPENERS** -- THOUGH AH SUPPOSE IN ITS ABSENCE...

SHKRANNG

...**GROKK'S TAIL 'LL** SUFFICE!

BY THE MIGHTY ONE --!

GOOD WORK, **HEX**.

CAREFUL, PEOPLE... AND WILL SOMEONE KEEP **ANGRY CHARLIE** FROM ACCIDENTALLY **DESTROYING** SOMETHING?

GROIK

I HOPE YOU'RE TELLING THE **TRUTH** THAT THE AGENDA IS KEEPING THEIR **CAPTIVES** HERE, **Ms. SPENCE**.

IF THIS IS SOME **TRICK** SO YOU CAN **ESCAPE**...

IF I COULD'VE **ESCAPED**, I WOULD'VE DONE IT **LONG** AGO, **GUARDIAN**.

I DON'T PARTICULARLY ENJOY LEE St. LAWRENCE'S **GUN BARREL** BREATHING DOWN MY **NECK**.

GRANT'S WORD!

SEE? EXACTLY AS **PROMISED**. ALL THE PROJECT'S SOLDIERS, SCIENTISTS AND STAFF -- IN **SUSPENDED ANIMATION**.

COMPLETELY **ALIVE** AND **UNHARMED**, IN CASE THEY WERE EVER NEEDED FOR... **FUTURE** EXPERIMENTS.

SIGH I SUPPOSE YOU'LL WANT ME TO **REVIVE** THEM ALL NOW...

-- YOU OKAY, MICKEY?
GETTIN' THERE! FEELS LIKE I GOT IRON STRAPPED TO MY WHOLE BODY -- NOT JUST MY ONE LEG.
ARE YOU SAYING -- GROWLER, ISN'T IT? -- ARE YOU SAYING THEY CLONED OVER A DOZEN OF ME TO HANDLE ADMINISTRATIVE DUTIES?
AT LEAST, Mrs. AVILIA.
Hmm... NOT A BAD IDEA!

EXCUSE ME...
COULD SOMEONE GIVE US A HAND?
TANA! SERLING!

WHAT ARE YOU TWO DOING HERE -- IT ISN'T SAFE! AND WHAT HAPPENED TO DUBBILEX?
Oh, YES -- WE WERE MUCH SAFER OUTSIDE -- WHERE THE GENE-GNOME TRIED TO KILL US! BUT DUBBILEX BROKE FREE FROM THE GNOME'S MENTAL CONTROL...

...RESULTING IN SEVERE CEREBRAL SHUTDOWN FOR BOTH. IF WE DON'T GET THEM ON LIFE SUPPORT, THEY COULD DIE!

ALL RIGHT, MEN -- DO WHATEVER DOCTOR ROQUETTE ASKS.
TAKE HIM TO MED-LAB SIX -- DOWN THE HALL ON THE RIGHT.

AS FOR YOU, Ms. MOON -- IT'S STILL EXTREMELY DANGEROUS IN HERE. YOU'LL HAVE TO BE ESCORTED OFF-PROJECT.
Oh, NO -- I'M NOT GOING ANYWHERE!

NOT ONLY DO I WANT TO ACTUALLY SEE THE AGENDA BE DEFEATED, BUT -- AFTER MONTHS AS THEIR PRISONER--
-- I NEED THIS STORY TO REESTABLISH MYSELF AS A JOURNALIST! AND YOU COULD USE A REPORTER ON YOUR SIDE TO STRAIGHTEN OUT THIS MESS, SO --

DON'T LOSE YOUR HEAD, TANA. AFTER ALL, IT WOULD BE... UNFORTUNATE IF ANYTHING HAPPENED TO SUPERBOY'S GIRLFRIEND.

I'D DIE HAPPY, AMANDA -- NOW THAT I'VE SEEN CHAINS ON YOU!
BUT WHERE'S SUPER --

BOY! NO ONE'S GUARDIN' THE GATES! THE WHOLE BROTHERHOOD OF EVIL INJUSTICE LEAGUE ASSASSINS COULD WALTZ RIGHT IN HERE!
'SUP?
KID!

EVERYTHING'S UNDER CONTROL, SUPERBOY. ALL THAT'S LEFT IS ROUNDING UP THE REMAINING CLONE-TROOPERS, AND THE CLONES OF MICKEY AND MYSELF.
SHOULDN'T BE A PROBLEM, NOW THAT YOU'RE --
I'M SO GLAD YOU'RE --

?!?
YOU'RE NOT SUPERBOY!

YOU SHOULDN'T HAVE SAID THAT, TANA.
WAM
I TRUST THAT ISN'T HOW SUPERBOY USUALLY GREETS HIS FRIENDS...
DAMN! SHOULD'VE REALIZED -- THE AGENDA DIDN'T CLONE SUPERBOY 'CAUSE THEY ALREADY HAD ONE...
...THE DOPPELGANGER CALLED MATCH!
YES. BUT THAT KNOWLEDGE WON'T HELP YOU, SINCE I HAVE ALL OF SUPERBOY'S POWERS -- AND MORE!
I'M GLAD YOU KNOW, ACTUALLY. I WON'T HAVE TO PRETEND TO BE THAT ANNOYING, BRASH --
C'MON, MATCH -- GIMME A BREAK!
GUESS I GOTTA PROVE THE REAL SUPERBOY'S -- DA BOMB!

ELSEWHERE IN THE PROJECT...
OUR NEWEST CREATIONS ARE VANISHING, MOKKARI! THE CONTESSA MUST BE RECALLING THEM! ABANDONING THE CADMUS OPERATION!
WE MUST CURRY HER FAVOR, SIMYAN! WE CAN BUT HOPE THAT DONOVAN HAS INVENTED SOMETHING TO DO SO!

INDEEDY--DEED I DID!
IF MY LOVELY ASSISTANT COULD HELP ME -- YOU ARE A CLONE OF DOCTOR ROCKET, CREATED BY THE AGENDA, AREN'T YOU?
YES...

SAY NO MORE! AND BELIEVE ME, YOU WILL SAY NO MORE -- EVER AGAIN!
GHEK--!
KTZZZH

AH! A THING OF BEAUTY, ISN'T IT? A VIRUS THAT ONLY AFFECTS AGENDA CLONES! SIMPLICITY, REALLY, ONCE I ISOLATED THEIR GENETIC SIGNATURE!
SADLY, THE VIRUS HAS ONLY A FEW MOMENTS' LIFE SPAN. WITH THIS DEADLINE, I HAD TO CHOOSE BETWEEN VIRULENCE AND LONGEVITY...
...BUT IT WILL TAKE OUT ALL THE AGENDA'S GENETIC JERKS INSIDE CADMUS! I APPRECIATE THEIR GOOD INTENTIONS -- I REALLY DO...

...BUT I SIMPLY CAN'T ALLOW ANYONE TO DESTROY THE PROJECT -- EXCEPT MYSELF!
THE HORROR, SIMYAN!

Oh, YOU'RE JUST JEALOUS!
BUT DON'T WORRY -- I HAVE A LITTLE SOMETHING FOR BOTH OF YOU!
PFSHHH

YOURS IS A FOOL'S FIGHT, SUPERBOY. YOU ARE IN NO CONDITION TO DEFEAT ME -- AND NONE WILL NOTICE WHEN I TAKE YOUR PLACE PERMANENTLY!
I'LL NOTICE, MATCH! DEEP DOWN -- I KNEW BEFORE! I SHOULD'VE FOLLOWED MY INSTINCTS! TIME TO FIX THAT MISTAKE!
YOUR MISTAKE, WONDER GIRL, IS NOT KNOWING I'M MORE THAN SIMPLY A CLONE OF SUPERBOY -- I'M AN IMPROVEMENT, WITH POWERS HE WILL NEVER POSSESS!
SUPERBOY AND WONDER GIRL ARE DOWN!
HEX, WILD MEN -- FOLLOW ME! WE HAVE TO STOP MATCH, OR --
YOU HAVE MORE TO WORRY ABOUT THAN JUST MATCH, GUARDIAN-ONE!
YOU SHOULDN'T BE SURPRISED. AFTER ALL, I ONLY DID WHAT YOU WOULD HAVE DONE IN THE SAME SITUATION.
MY TROOPS AND I FLANKED YOUR POSITION...

"...TO LAUNCH AN ATTACK FROM AN UNEXPECTED DIRECTION!"
GIVE 'EM ALL YOU GOT! WE GO DOWN -- WE GO IN A BLAZE OF GLORY!

I BELIEVE THE TIDE IS TURNING, WONDER GIRL.
DON'T WORRY. I SENSED A CERTAIN... ATTRACTION BETWEEN YOU AND SUPERBOY. I'M SURE THE AGENDA WILL CLONE YOU INTO MY PERFECT COUNTER-PART!
WON'T DO... ANY GOOD! MY MOTHER'LL NEVER APPROVE OF YOU!

DIDN'T KNOW --
NG!
--DIDN'T KNOW "MATCH" WAS SHORT... FOR "MATCHMAKER!" BUT IF CASSIE... EVER GOES WITH ANY SUPERBOY... IT'S GONNA BE THE... REAL DEAL!
SO QUIT... NECKING!

I DON'T KNOW HOW THE AGENDA TWISTED ME TO GET YOU, PAL -- BUT I WON'T LET THEM TWIST THAT SHIELD TO SERVE AND PROTECT NEO-NAZIS!
KWOK

THRANG
OUR BATTLE IS ALREADY OVER, SUPERBOY.
YOU AREN'T MY MATCH -- EVEN AT YOUR STRONGEST!

YEAH! WE... WE ARE DIFFERENT!
THAT'S... THE POINT!
THAK

SO YOU ADMIT I'M YOUR BETTER. THEN WHY CONTINUE THIS USELESS STRUGGLE? IT MAKES NO SENSE.
UNZAAK

YOU DON'T... GET IT. YOU'VE DONE WHAT THE AGENDA WANTS... BEEN WHO THE AGENDA WANTS... BUT...
YOU GOT... NO IDEA WHAT IT MEANS TO... BE YOUR OWN PERSON!
ME, I... I DON'T HAVE A MOTHER OR... OR FATHER, OR ANY MEMORIES OF GROWIN' UP. ALL -- KH -- ALL I GOT IS WHO I AM.

YOU STOLE THAT FROM ME -- AND I WANT IT BACK!
GET A LIFE -- BUT NOT MINE! YOU AREN'T SUPERBOY!
YOU'LL NEVER BE SUPERBOY!
KREK

YOU'RE RIGHT. I SEE EVERYTHING SO CLEARLY NOW.
THERE. SATISFIED?
YOU... YOU'RE GIVIN' UP?

HARDLY.

I'VE SIMPLY TAKEN AWAY YOUR REASON TO CONTINUE FIGHTING!
KWOK

HEX! GIVE ME A HAND HERE!
NO, HEX! I'M THE REAL GUARDIAN -- NOT HIM!
WELL, NOW -- IT'S A MITE HARD TA FIGURE WHICH OF YOU HOMBRES IS TELLIN' THE TRUTH.
SO AH SUGGEST NEITHER OF YOU MAKE ANY SUDDEN MOVES!

LEAVE HIM! CAN'T YOU SEE HE'S HAD ENOUGH?!
JUST... JUST GETTIN' MY... SECOND WIND... TANA...
OUT OF THE WAY, WOMAN.
THE AGENDA HAS OTHER PLANS FOR YOU...

FORGET THE AGENDA, MATCH! KILL THEM BO--
KHUFF KEHK
HEGK --!
WHAT'S HAPPENING? WHAT'S HAPPENING?

MASSIVE, INSTANTANEOUS D.N.A. DISINTEGRATION. A CLONE VIRUS.
I'M AFRAID WE'LL HAVE TO SETTLE OUR MATTERS LATER, SUPERBOY...
AAA --!

...ASSUMING YOU SURVIVE.

...**NO ONE** DESERVES TO DIE LIKE **THIS!**

NO ONE...

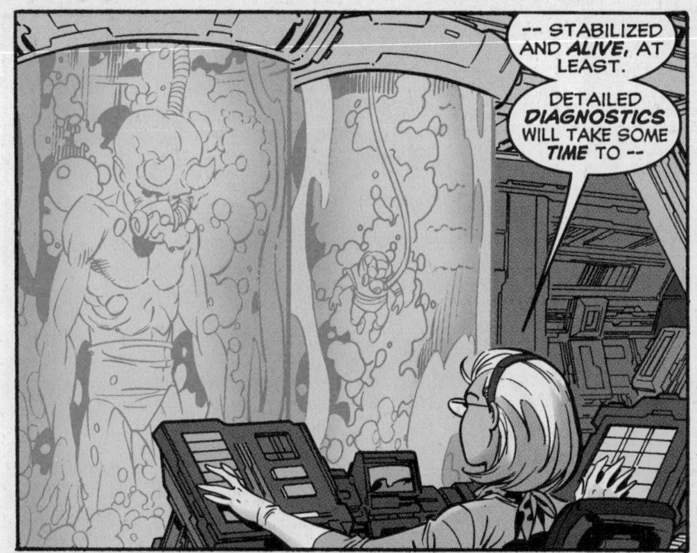
-- STABILIZED AND ALIVE, AT LEAST.
DETAILED DIAGNOSTICS WILL TAKE SOME TIME TO --

SERLING! THERE'S SOME STRANGE... GAS KILLING OFF HALF THE PEOPLE OUT THERE!
I'VE GOT THE DOOR, TANA -- GET SUPERBOY ON THE EXAMINING TABLE!

WAS... WAS HE EXPOSED?
I DON'T THINK SO. THERE WAS SOMETHING WRONG WITH HIM BEFORE -- HE'S IN BAD SHAPE!

DON'T... DON'T WORRY... TANA. PROB'LY JUST... BRUISED MY... EGO...
DOC'LL TAKE... GOOD CARE OF... ME. SO THINK I'LL JUST... PASS... OUT...
REST EASY, KID. I'LL BE HERE WHEN YOU WAKE UP.

YOU... YOU LOVE HIM, DON'T YOU?
WELL, WE'VE BEEN THROUGH A LOT TOGETHER. FROM THE FIRST DAY HE SHOWED UP, TO HIM BEING STUCK AT SIXTEEN, TO... TO NOW.
YES. I DO LOVE HIM.

DO YOU?

GOOD NEWS, GIRLS -- SENSORS INDICATE ALL CLEAR. THAT STUFF DISAPPEARED FAST AS THE FLASH! MIND IF WE JOIN YOU?
ACTUALLY, I COULD WORK ON SUPERBOY BETTER WITHOUT DISTRACTIONS, SIR. SO, UM, IF TANA DOESN'T MIND...?

OF COURSE NOT. I'LL WAIT OUTSIDE WITH THE OTHERS. JUST HELP HIM.
I'LL DO EVERYTHING I CAN -- AND ANYTHING I HAVE TO...

AND THE FIRST THING I HAVE TO DO IS GET A BIO-SCAN TO ASSESS --
WHAT --? THIS CAN'T BE!
HE'S BEING TORN APART ON A GENETIC LEVEL!

I'VE NEVER SEEN DATA LIKE THIS! I DON'T EVEN KNOW WHERE TO BEGIN!
SUPERBOY COULD DIE!

-- SAVED MY LIFE MORE THAN ONCE. DON'T KNOW WHAT I'D DO WITHOUT THE KID...
KON-EL.

Hm?
HIS NAME'S KON-EL. ALL HIS FRIENDS CALL HIM THAT.
Oh! I... I DIDN'T --

NO WORRIES, TANA...

...I THINK I'M GOING TO HAVE TO HAVE EVERYONE START CALLING ME SOMETHING ELSE, ANYWAY!
SOME SORT OF... AGING FORCE WAS AT WAR WITH HIS STUCK-AT-SIXTEEN CELLULAR STRUCTURE.
THEN IT, Um... CAME TO ME HOW TO ALTER HIS D.N.A. SO THE CELLS WEREN'T CHRONOLOGICALLY STALLED, AND... END OF PROBLEM!
WELL, ONE PROBLEM, AT LEAST!

SUPER... BOY?
DON'T LET THE CAPE FOOL YOU, MICKEY. I DON'T KNOW WHERE IT CAME FROM, EITHER!
IT JUST APPEARED LIKE... MAGIC!

A MIRACLE IS MORE LIKE IT! I'M SO GLAD YOU'RE OKAY, KID!
I MEAN -- KON-EL... OR SUPERMAN... OR --
WE'LL HAVE PLENTY OF TIME TO SORT IT OUT, TANA --

HOW TOUCHING. YOU CAN'T IMAGINE HOW LONG I'VE WAITED FOR THIS MOMENT.
BY THE WAY -- NICE NECKLACE, TANA. I BELIEVE THE AGENDA GAVE YOU THAT. A SORT OF... GOING AWAY PRESENT.
TOK

AAA--!
TANA!

MY GOD.
SHE'S DEAD.
NO.
NO! THERE MUST BE A WAY TO SAVE HER... BRING HER BACK... CLONE HER!

HER MIND'S GONE, SUPERBOY! WE COULDN'T RETRIEVE HER MEMORIES! SHE WOULDN'T BE THE SAME PERSON!
IS THAT WHAT SHE WOULD WANT? IS THAT WHAT YOU REALLY WANT?

IT IS BEST SERVED COLD, ISN'T IT, LEE?
YOU SEE, MY FATHER WAS PAUL WESTFIELD. I WORSHIPPED HIM, BUT HE WAS KILLED AND ALL THAT WAS LEFT WAS A PATHETIC CLONE OF HIM NAMED SUPERBOY!
SO I PLOTTED, AND WAITED, AND KILLED SOMEONE SUPERBOY LOVED IN RETURN. NOW HE CAN BEGIN TO UNDERSTAND MY PAIN!
SUPERBOY, I'M SORRY! I --

NO, LEE...

...SPENCE IS THE ONE WHO'S GOING TO BE SORRY!
FSHROOM

THANKS FOR THE SAVE, LEE -- NOT THAT I NEEDED IT!
REMEMBER EARLIER WHEN I SAID I COULDN'T ESCAPE? I LIED!

THIS CAN'T BE HAPPENING...
NONE OF THIS CAN BE HAPPENING...
SUPERBOY, IF... THERE'S ANYTHING I CAN --

GIVE HIM A MOMENT ALONE, SERLING. SUPERBOY JUST LOST A BIG PART OF HIS YOUTH...

"...AND IT WASN'T BECAUSE HE WAS TRANSFORMED INTO A MAN."

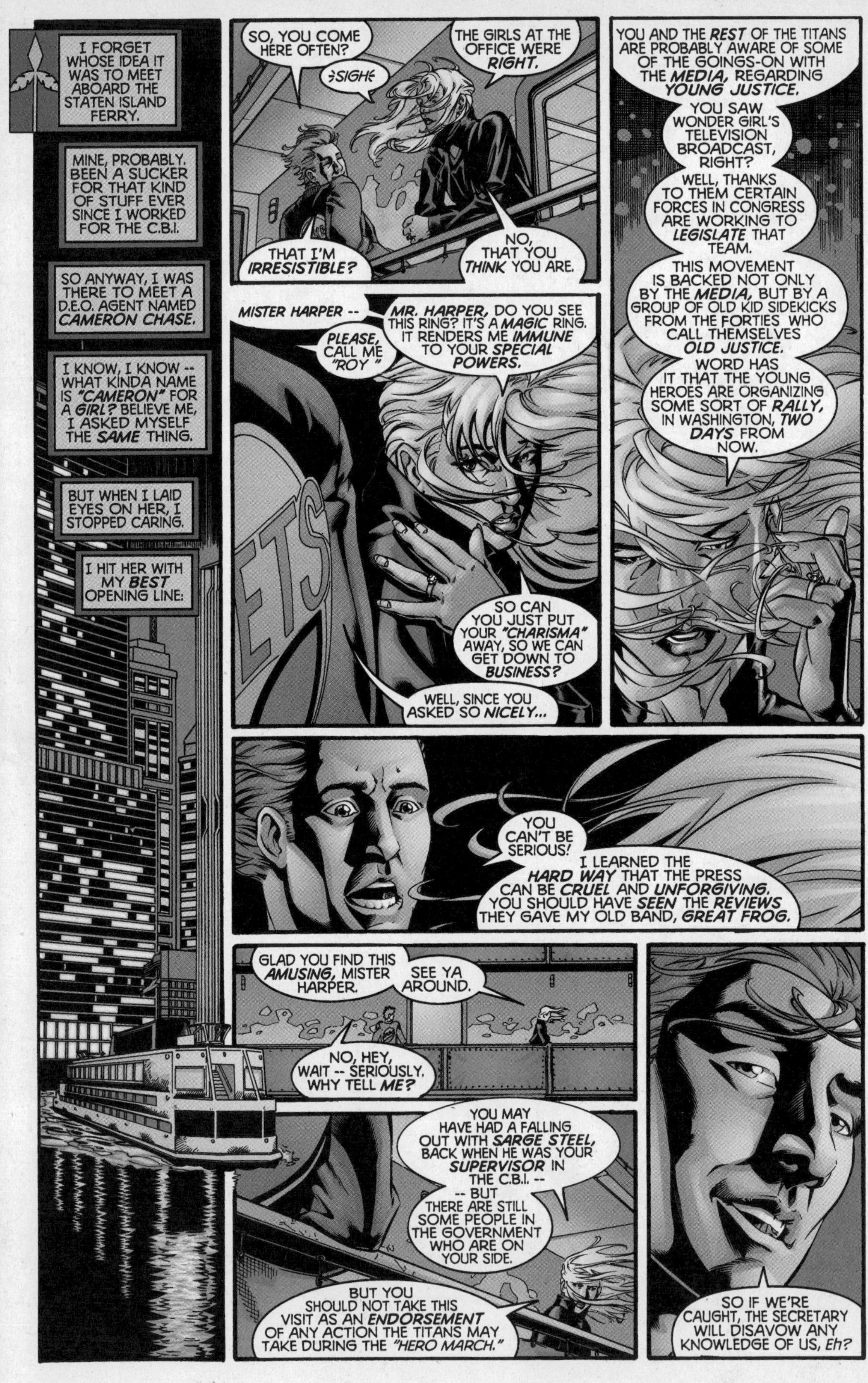
I FORGET WHOSE IDEA IT WAS TO MEET ABOARD THE STATEN ISLAND FERRY.
MINE, PROBABLY. BEEN A SUCKER FOR THAT KIND OF STUFF EVER SINCE I WORKED FOR THE C.B.I.
SO ANYWAY, I WAS THERE TO MEET A D.E.O. AGENT NAMED CAMERON CHASE.
I KNOW, I KNOW -- WHAT KINDA NAME IS "CAMERON" FOR A GIRL? BELIEVE ME, I ASKED MYSELF THE SAME THING.
BUT WHEN I LAID EYES ON HER, I STOPPED CARING.
I HIT HER WITH MY BEST OPENING LINE:
SO, YOU COME HERE OFTEN?
SIGH
THE GIRLS AT THE OFFICE WERE RIGHT.
THAT I'M IRRESISTIBLE?
NO, THAT YOU THINK YOU ARE.
MISTER HARPER --
PLEASE, CALL ME "ROY"
MR. HARPER, DO YOU SEE THIS RING? IT'S A MAGIC RING. IT RENDERS ME IMMUNE TO YOUR SPECIAL POWERS.
SO CAN YOU JUST PUT YOUR "CHARISMA" AWAY, SO WE CAN GET DOWN TO BUSINESS?
WELL, SINCE YOU ASKED SO NICELY...
YOU AND THE REST OF THE TITANS ARE PROBABLY AWARE OF SOME OF THE GOINGS-ON WITH THE MEDIA, REGARDING YOUNG JUSTICE.
YOU SAW WONDER GIRL'S TELEVISION BROADCAST, RIGHT?
WELL, THANKS TO THEM CERTAIN FORCES IN CONGRESS ARE WORKING TO LEGISLATE THAT TEAM.
THIS MOVEMENT IS BACKED NOT ONLY BY THE MEDIA, BUT BY A GROUP OF OLD KID SIDEKICKS FROM THE FORTIES WHO CALL THEMSELVES OLD JUSTICE.
WORD HAS IT THAT THE YOUNG HEROES ARE ORGANIZING SOME SORT OF RALLY, IN WASHINGTON, TWO DAYS FROM NOW.
YOU CAN'T BE SERIOUS!
I LEARNED THE HARD WAY THAT THE PRESS CAN BE CRUEL AND UNFORGIVING. YOU SHOULD HAVE SEEN THE REVIEWS THEY GAVE MY OLD BAND, GREAT FROG.
GLAD YOU FIND THIS AMUSING, MISTER HARPER.
SEE YA AROUND.
NO, HEY, WAIT -- SERIOUSLY. WHY TELL ME?
YOU MAY HAVE HAD A FALLING OUT WITH SARGE STEEL, BACK WHEN HE WAS YOUR SUPERVISOR IN THE C.B.I. --
-- BUT THERE ARE STILL SOME PEOPLE IN THE GOVERNMENT WHO ARE ON YOUR SIDE.
BUT YOU SHOULD NOT TAKE THIS VISIT AS AN ENDORSEMENT OF ANY ACTION THE TITANS MAY TAKE DURING THE "HERO MARCH."
SO IF WE'RE CAUGHT, THE SECRETARY WILL DISAVOW ANY KNOWLEDGE OF US, Eh?

SO WE WENT TO THE "JUSTICE FOR ALL" RALLY.
AND THINGS GOT KINDA...
...CRAZY.
Disaffected YOUTH
JAY FAERBER story
MIKE MILLER & NORM BREYFOGLE pencils
WALDEN WONG & SCOTT KOBLISH inks
TOM McCRAW colors
DIGITAL CHAMLEON separations
COMICRAFT letters
MAUREEN McTIGU editor
X'HAL!
I'VE... I'VE BEEN CHANGED! MADE... YOUNGER! AND SO HAS VICTOR!
AND ARGENT AND I... WE'RE... WE'RE... ADULTS!
YO, CHECK IT.
AND WE WEREN'T AFFECTED AT ALL!
BUT WHY...?

SO THAT'S WHAT BRINGS US HERE TO S.T.A.R. LABS, SARAH.
AFTER THE DUST CLEARED, ALL THE HEROES SPLIT UP, EACH HOPING TO FIND A WAY TO REVERSE THIS AGE-THING.
FLASH... I MEAN, KID FLASH... WENT OFF WITH THE JLA, WHICH IS WHY HE ISN'T WITH US.
SHE'D BETTER! I MISS BEING... TALLER.
CYBORG, WILL YOU PLEASE STOP STARING AT ME.
MMMM MMMM!
F-I-N-E FINE!
I... I DON'T KNOW WHERE TO START! I SUPPOSE I SHOULD BE USED TO THIS SORT OF THING BY NOW --
-- CONSIDERING HOW LONG I'VE KNOWN YOU ALL, BUT YOU'VE JUST GOT TO GIVE ME A MINUTE, HERE.
DONNA?
YES, GARTH?
IT'S DAYS LIKE THIS I WONDER WHY I EVER CAME ASHORE.
COME ON, YOU GUYS. WE NEED TO PULL IT TOGETHER, HERE.
WE AGREED TO MEET BACK AT THE YOUNG JUSTICE HQ LATER ON, ONCE WE'VE GOTTEN OUR BEARINGS.
SO CAN YOU HELP US?
COME ON, TONI. YOU HEARD THE MAN. WE NEED TO GET...
...TOGETHER.
PLEASE MAKE HIM STOP.
HA! LI'L VIC'S A HOUND DOG!
THIS IS SO... UNSETTLING. I NEVER KNEW VIC WAS SUCH A... LEWD KID.
I HEAR YA.
MAN, TONI OVER THERE'S GOT A BIG FUTURE AHEAD OF HER.
SARAH... ROY... A LITTLE FOCUS HERE, PLEASE.
THE WAY I SEE IT, OUR PROBLEM IS TWO-FOLD.
WE NEED TO FIGURE OUT HOW TO "FIX" DAMAGE, ARGENT, CYBORG AND STARFIRE --
-- AND FIGURE OUT WHY TEMPEST, TROIA, ARSENAL AND I WEREN'T AFFECTED.
I LOVE IT WHEN YOU'RE THINKING!
MMMMM-WA!

UM... AHEM...
WHAT? YOU USED TO LIKE IT WHEN I DID THAT.
KORY --

I BEG YOUR PARDON! I WILL BE ADDRESSED AS PRINCESS KORIAND'R... OR NOT AT ALL!
HA HA HA... Oh, MAN -- BALL'S IN YOUR COURT, FEARLESS LEADER!
...

KOR... Um, PRINCESS --
SHUT UP. YOU'RE UGLY. I'M THE PRETTIEST ONE HERE!

SOOO... REMIND ME AGAIN WHY YOU TWO BROKE UP?
Shhhh, GARTH!

I HAVE SAT AND WATCHED THIS PETTY BICKERING LONG ENOUGH!
WE NEED TO PUT OUR DIFFERENCES ASIDE AND GET TO THE ROOT OF THE PROBLEM.
PERHAPS IF WE CAN DETERMINE WHY THE ORIGINAL TITANS WEREN'T AFFECTED, WE CAN USE THAT KNOWLEDGE TO FORMULATE SOME SORT OF CURE.

YOU KNOW WHAT? DAMAGE IS RIGHT. AND SOMETHING HE JUST SAID MADE ME REMEMBER SOMETHING...

"IT WAS A WHILE AGO, JUST AFTER WE'D FORMED THE ORIGINAL TEEN TITANS.
"THE TEENAGERS OF A TOWN CALLED EDEN CREST ASKED US TO PROVIDE SECURITY FOR A ROCK CONCERT.
"I GUESS WE WERE THE ONLY ONES BOTH THE KIDS AND THE ADULTS COULD AGREE ON.
"THE PERFORMER WAS A GUY NAMED LIMBO. I DON'T KNOW WHAT'S HAPPENED TO HIM SINCE, BUT BACK THEN, HE WAS THE HOTTEST ROCK STAR AROUND.
"KIDS LOVED HIM, AND ADULTS, WELL, ADULTS WERE AFRAID OF THE EFFECT HE HAD ON THEIR KIDS.
"TURNS OUT THEY HAD A GOOD REASON TO BE, BECAUSE BY THE TIME LIMBO WAS INTO HIS SECOND SONG, THE CROWD WAS LITERALLY GOING WILD
"AND WONDER GIRL, SPEEDY, KID FLASH, AQUALAD, AND I WERE TRYING TO KEEP THINGS UNDER CONTROL."
LIMBO
THAT'S IT TEAM! JUST KEEP THE KIDS ISOLATED!
THAT'S EASY FOR YOU TO SAY, ROBIN! THESE CATS ARE OUT OF CONTROL!
JUST DO WHAT I DO, WONDER-CHICK -- STAY ONE STEP AHEAD OF 'EM!
NO ONE LIKES A SHOW-OFF, KID FLASH!
THERE'S TOO MANY OF THEM!
I DON'T KNOW IF WE CAN STOP THEM ALL!
I STEPPED ON YOUR DOG!
YOUR MOMMA'S A HOG!
"AQUALAD WAS RIGHT. THERE WERE TOO MANY OF THEM.
"AND THEN THINGS GOT WORSE."
WREEEOOOOOE

"THE RIOT HAD GROWN SO OUT OF CONTROL THAT BOTH THE LOCAL POLICE AND THE NATIONAL GUARD WERE CALLED IN --
"--WHICH WAS GOING TO MAKE A VOLATILE SITUATION TURN EXPLOSIVE IF WE DIDN'T ACT FAST.
WREEEOOO WREEEOOO
SKREECH
NATIONAL GUARD
POLICE
TITANS! THE AUTHORITIES HAVE JUST SHOWN UP IN FULL FORCE!
WE CAN'T LET THE TROOPS INJURE THE KIDS!
WE NEED TO CONTAIN THIS SITUATION, BEFORE --
"IT WAS TOO LATE. THE KIDS REACTED AS I FEARED THEY WOULD, ATTACKING EVERYTHING IN SIGHT.
KSSHH
POLICE
"AND THE NATIONAL GUARD RETALIATED WITH TEAR GAS.
PFAF
PFAF
PFAF
KID FLASH, YOU CAN --
ALREADY ON IT, BAT-BOY!
I CAN WHIP US UP A WHIRLWIND TO DISSIPATE THE GAS!
WOOOOSH

THIS IS *CRAZY,* MAN!

OOF

ROBBIE, WE NEED TO GET LIMBO OFF THE STAGE! HE'S IN *DANGER* UP THERE!

I KNOW, *SPEEDY,* I KNOW. HE'S A SITTING DUCK AS LONG AS HE'S... *WAITAMINUTE...*

WHY *IS* HE STILL UP THERE? WHY HASN'T HE RUN FOR *COVER?* DOES HE HAVE A *DEATH WISH,* OR... **OH NO!**

ON IT, LEADER MAN. BE BACK IN A -- WELL, YOU KNOW.

WHOOOAA...
WHAT'S THIS?
ROBIN, IT'S KID FLASH. I'M A COUPLE MILES OUTSIDE TOWN, AND I THINK I FOUND WHAT YOU WERE LOOKING FOR.
IT'S ONE CRAZY SCENE. THE CARDY RESEARCH CENTER IS BEING OVERRUN WITH ARMED GOONS.
I KNEW IT! THIS ENTIRE RIOT WAS JUST A DISTRACTION!
JUST HOLD TIGHT, KID FLASH. WE'LL BE THERE ASAP!
SPEEDY! I NEED YOU TO TAKE OUT LIMBO'S SOUND SYSTEM -- NOW!
Aww, MAN! IT'S A CRIME TO RUIN A PERFECTLY GOOD SETUP LIKE THAT!

IT'S A TOUGH JOB...
...BUT SOMEBODY'S GOTTA DO IT.
TWANG
FZZZT
IT WORKED! SPEEDY DID IT!
SEE THAT, AQUALAD? SHE KNOWS THE SCORE.
KEEP DREAMING, FEATHERHEAD.
"WE DIDN'T KNOW IT AT THE TIME, BUT LIMBO SLIPPED AWAY WHILE EVERYONE WAS REGAINING THEIR SENSES."
ROBIN! WHAT HAPPENED HERE?!
I'M NOT SURE, SIR... ...BUT I THINK LIMBO MIGHT'VE BEEN THE CAUSE OF IT --
-- LITERALLY.
SOME OF THESE KIDS MAY NEED MEDICAL ATTENTION, BUT THE WORST IS OVER.
ROBIN! I'M DOING AN AERIAL SEARCH FOR LIMBO --

-- BUT I CAN'T SEEM TO FIND HIM *ANYWHERE!* HE JUST ***VANISHED!***

BLAST IT! KID FLASH COULD PROBABLY FIND HIM WITH A *SUPER-SPEED SEARCH,* BUT WE NEED HIM WHERE HE IS --

"-- HOLDING DOWN THE FORT AT THE RESEARCH CENTER!"

CARDY RESEARCH CENTER

HANG ON, POPS!

DO YOU KNOW WHAT THESE CLOWNS ARE *AFTER?*

YOU WEREN'T GOING TO SHOOT ANYONE WITH THAT...
...WERE YOU?
PASH
TWANG
HA! YOU GUYS SEE THAT? THAT GUY'S NOT SURE IF HE'S IN LOVE WITH WONDY OR SCARED TO DEATH OF HER!
I GOTTA ADMIT, PALLY, I CAN RELATE!
ENOUGH CHATTER, TEAM. LET'S TAKE 'EM OUT!
BONK
KRACK
HNGH
ROBBIE, THE TROOPS HAVE MADE IT INTO THE BUILDING!
WHACK WHACK WHACK
OKAY, KID FLASH, YOU STAY OUT HERE, AND KEEP ANY MORE TROOPS FROM MAKING IT INSIDE.
THE REST OF YOU ARE WITH ME!

ANYBODY HOME?
SLUNNK
KRRASSSHH
THEY'RE SIPHONING OFF THE GAS!
A YOUTH SERUM COULD TIP THE BALANCE OF POWER ON A GLOBAL SCALE!
THEN I GUESS WE'D BETTER PUT A STOP TO THIS, Eh?
BRAAT
HA! MISSED ME!
WHUD
SPEEDY, NO!
KRUSH
HSSSHHHHHH
"THE BLAST THAT WAS MEANT FOR SPEEDY HIT THE GLASS DOME THAT HOUSED THE RETARDING CHEMICALS.
"WE MANAGED TO CONTAIN THE REST OF THE TROOPS, AND WE WERE ALL CHECKED OUT BY DOCTORS.
"NO ONE SUFFERED ANY SIDE EFFECTS FROM INHALING THE CHEMICAL FORMULA.

"BUT WE NEVER DID FIND OUT WHAT HAPPENED TO LIMBO, THOUGH."

BLAST IT, CONTESSA! YOU PROMISED ME THAT IF I MADE A BIG ENOUGH *DISTRACTION*, WE'D *BOTH* GET WHAT WE WANTED.

YOU'D GET YOUR FANCY *ANTI-AGING* FORMULA, AND I'D GET TO HAVE SOME *FUN* WITH A BUNCH OF *ANGRY KIDS*.

SO THOSE CHEMICALS THE FOUR OF YOU INHALED COULD HAVE MADE YOU IMMUNE TO WHATEVER ALTERED THE AGES OF EVERYONE ELSE.
OF COURSE! THE ANTIDOTE IS IN YOUR BLOOD!
THAT'S EXACTLY WHAT I WAS THINKING. I JUST HOPE WE CAN ISOLATE WHAT IT IS BEFORE IT'S TOO LATE.
I'LL GET STARTED PROCESSING THE DATA. VIC, COULD YOU --
YEAH, MOMMA? WHAT D'YA NEED?
NEVER MIND.
SARAH! EVERYONE! TURN ON THE NEWS, QUICK!
Oh, LOOKIT WHO IT IS. DESHAUN, THE LOVE OF SARAH'S LIFE. WUZZUP?
Um, DON'T MIND HIM, DESHAUN. WHAT'S GOING ON?
DONNA, THAT MONITOR DOUBLES AS A TV.
-- COSTUMED TERRORISTS KNOWN AS THE WILDEBEESTS ARE LAUNCHING AN ASSAULT ON JFK INTERNATIONAL AIRPORT.
THE WILDEBEESTS?! I THOUGHT WE'D SEEN THE LAST OF THEM!
WE HAVE TO STOP THEM! THEY'RE OUR RESPONSIBILITY!
BUT IF WE LEAVE, SARAH WON'T BE ABLE TO MAKE THAT ANTIDOTE!
AND DON'T FORGET WE'RE SUPPOSED TO MEET BACK AT YOUNG JUSTICE'S HQ.
WE'RE HEROES. WE'VE SWORN TO PROTECT ALL MANKIND.
WITH THAT IN MIND, WE HAVE NO CHOICE BUT TO LAUNCH OURSELVES INTO ACTION! ARE YOU WITH ME?
WOW.
THAT'S MY BOY!

I THINK I LIKE BEING AN ADULT, DONNA!
WHEN I WAS A KID, MY POWERS WERE TOO UNCONTROLLABLE TO FLY LIKE THIS.
YOU'VE SURE GOT YOUR ACT TOGETHER, GRANT. NO ONE'S DENYING THAT!
CYBORG, TEMPEST -- THERE ARE PEOPLE ABOARD THAT PLANE.
STOP THE 'BEESTS AND HELP EVACUATE THE PASSENGERS!
I HEAR YOU, BRO'.
I'VE WAITED FOR THIS DAY TO COME!
HOLD ON, PEEPS. GONNA HELP CUT Y'ALL OUTTA THERE!
BUTCHERS! DO YOU REMEMBER ME?
YOU ALMOST KILLED ME!

THERE IT IS! YOU HAVE A PLAN, NIGHTWING?
OF COURSE HE HAS A PLAN. THAT'S LIKE ASKING IF I HAVE MY SUNGLASSES.
GET US OVER THE PLANE THAT'S SMOKING, OVER THERE.
YOU KILLED MY FRIEND! ①
① GOLDEN EAGLE, BACK IN NEW TITANS #72.
JUST ABOUT THERE, FOLKS. I'M MAKING YOU ANOTHER WAY OUT.
THEY'RE EVERYWHERE! MY GOD, THEY'RE EVERYWHERE!

THIS WAY, YO!

WALK, DON'T RUN, TO YOUR NEAREST CYBORG!

HANG ON, DAMAGE! I'M COMING!

THERE!
WITHOUT THEIR EXOSKELETONS, THESE WILDEBEESTS ARE JUST NORMAL --

GREAT HERA!

THESE WILDEBEESTS AREN'T *MEN* IN *COSTUMES* -- THEY'RE... THEY'RE *REAL MONSTERS!*
THEY'VE ALWAYS BEEN *MONSTERS* TO *ME.*
THESE 'BEESTS SEEM A LOT *TOUGHER* THAN WHEN THEY WERE JUST GUYS IN *SUITS,* TEAM.
WE MAY NEED TO BEEF UP OUR ASSAULT.
Oh, REALLY?
SO I GUESS WE DON'T NEED TO *HOLD BACK* ANYMORE, Eh?
SKREEE
KA BLAMMM

I GUESS THIS IS --
-UGH-
-- ONE TIME WHEN KORY'S BLOODLUST WILL COME IN HANDY.
I DON'T KNOW THAT I'M COMFORTABLE EVER --
-ENH-
-- CONDONING HER RUTHLESSNESS.
YA-HOO! LOOKING GOOD, GRANT!
I'M STARTING TO LIKE THIS!
WHAT, KICKING WILDEBEEST TAIL?
NO.
BEING AN ADULT.
I'M NOT SURE I WANT A CURE.
WELL, THAT'S A LOADED ISSUE THERE, KIDDO. I DON'T THINK YOU SHOULD --
WHA --?
GREAT SCOTT!

THE WILDEBEESTS ARE DESTROYING THE CONTROL TOWER!

WITHOUT IT, INCOMING PLANES WON'T KNOW WHAT'S GOING ON! THEY COULD COME LANDING RIGHT INTO THE MIDDLE OF THIS NIGHTMARE!

STARFIRE! WITH ME!

I NEED YOU TO BLAST THE WILDEBEESTS OFF THE TOWER, ***NO MATTER WHAT.***

NOW THAT'S THE KIND OF LEADER I LIKE!
ARGENT! I NEED YOU TO USE YOUR POWERS TO BUILD A SIGN!

A SIGN? HEY, I SEE WHERE YOU'RE GOING WITH THAT. VERY CLEVER!

I'M NOT SURE THIS IS GOING TO WORK, GRANT. WHAT IF IT ISN'T BIG ENOUGH?
YOU'LL JUST HAVE TO MAKE SURE IT IS BIG ENOUGH!

DANGER!! TURN BACK
WHOA! IS THAT FOR REAL?
CAN WE TAKE A CHANCE THAT IT'S NOT?

I SHOULD SNAP YOUR NECK, LIKE YOU DID TO CHARLIE...

EASY, GILL-HEAD. WE'RE THE GOOD GUYS, 'MEMBER?

Oooooh, MAN! WHAT A SCRAP! I'M GONNA BE SORE FOR A WEEK.
ANY VOLUNTEERS TO RUB ON THE MUSCLE RELAXANT?
NYC
THX 1138
DON'T LOOK AT ME, HARPER.
GOOD WORK, TEAM. I JUST DID A FLYBY, AND THE DAMAGE TO THE AIRPORT ISN'T AS BAD AS IT LOOKS.
I CAN'T BELIEVE HOW MANY THERE WERE.
OR HOW STRONG THEY WERE.
OR HOW BAD THEY STANK.

THERE THEY ARE. THE TITANS. YOU BELIEVE ALL THAT STUFF THEY KEEP SAYING ABOUT THOSE SUPER-KIDS ON TV?
SURE DO. ALWAYS DID THINK THOSE KIDS DO MORE HARM THAN GOOD.
Aw, COME ON, MORTY.
THEY SAVED OUR REARS HUNDREDS OF TIMES.
WELL, NOW WE CAN TRY TO MEET UP WITH THE OTHER HEROES, AND SEE IF THEY HAVE A CURE FOR OUR CONDITION.
NOT SO FAST...

HI, I'M DETECTIVE QUINN -- I HATE TO BE THE BEARER OF BAD NEWS, BUT WE JUST GOT WORD THAT THERE ARE MORE OF THESE WILDEBEESTS ATTACKING GRAND CENTRAL STATION!

THERE'S... MORE... OF THEM?
Oh... MOMMA.

ELSEWHERE...
Oh DEAR, IT LOOKS LIKE THE TITANS WON'T BE GETTING ANY REST FOR THE NEXT COUPLE OF DAYS.
I SEEM TO RECALL YOU WEREN'T VERY HAPPY WITH THE OUTCOME OF OUR PREVIOUS PARTNERSHIP.
DOES THIS SUIT YOU ANY BETTER... GRUNGE, OR RAVE, OR GOTH, OR WHATEVER IT IS YOU CALL YOURSELF TODAY?
IT MOST CERTAINLY DOES, CONTESSA. THE TITANS MAY HAVE DISMISSED ME WHEN WE MET IN EDEN CREST ALL THOSE YEARS AGO --
-- BUT I'M SURE THEY'D THINK OTHERWISE IF THEY KNEW I WAS THE ONE WHO "UPGRADED" THE WILDEBEESTS.

WOULD YOU GUYS GROW UP?!?
CRISIS ON INFANTILE EARTHS
GEOFFY JOHNS & BENNY RABB words
KIDDIE CARLO BARBERI - pencils
LI'L WADE VON G - inks
TOMMY McCRAW - colors
BILLY OAKLEY - letters
THIS CLUBHOUSE IS JLA ONLY.
YEAH, AND THAT MEANS NO ADULT DIAPERS ALLOWED!
HEY, THEM'S FIGHTIN' WORDS.

Y'KNOW, STARWOMAN, I CAN DIVE FOR HOURS WITHOUT HAVING TO COME UP FOR AIR.
GO BACK TO THE AQUARIUM, SHRIMP. WE'VE GOT A CRISIS HERE.
IF WE DON'T GET SOME ROCKET FUEL FOR OUR SHIP WE'LL NEVER GET TO THE PLANET MYRG.
GOD, I REALLY DON'T WANT TO GO INTO SPACE.

SO WHAT?
SO WHAT? THAT'S WHERE MY PAL, DOIBY DICKLES, HAS ANOTHER ONE OF THOSE DE-AGING GUNS.
DOIBY DICKLES? YEAH, SOME PAL.
CRYBABY SANG LIKE A CANARY ABOUT THE SECRET STASH OF ROCKET FUEL YOU GUYS KEEP IN CASE OF EMERGENCIES.
LOUD-MOUTH.
HEY, I BET STEEL HAS PLENTY OF ROCKET FUEL IN THOSE BOOTS OF HIS.
THAT'S NOT VERY FAIR, IS IT, TERRIFIC LAD?
FAIR, SHMAIRE. HE'S TOAST.
YEAH, S.T.R.I.P.E.S.Y. LET'S DOUBLE-TEAM HIM.
?

LOOK, DOOFUS, I WAS A FOUNDING MEMBER OF THE JLA.
AND I WORKED WITH 'EM FOR AWHILE TOO, RUNT. SO GET OUTTA MY WAY!
WHAT PART OF "CURRENT JLA MEMBERS ONLY" DON'T YOU UNDERSTAND?
OH, C'MON. YOU'VE ONLY BEEN A MEMBER FOR, LIKE, A WEEK!
!

WHO CARES? THE JLA'S LAME ANYWAY. THE JSA IS WHERE IT'S AT! THE JLA IS SO... MAINSTREAM.
COME ON, EVERYONE. WE'VE GOT TO WORK TOGETHER ...UNLESS YOU WANT TO STAY LIKE THIS FOREVER!
DON'T MATTER TO ME. I'M HAVIN' A KICKIN' TIME.

I'LL SAY.
BOING!
ENUFFA THIS YAKKIN'. C'MON, BOYS--

AND GIRLS!
WHATEVER.
LET'S BUST SOME HEADS!
I'M IN HELL.
HEY, WATCH THE LANGUAGE. WE'RE SUPERHEROES, REMEMBER?
OOH, LOOK AT ME! I'M AN ALIEN AND I'M SO SCARED OF FIRE!
GEEK.
BETTERSLOWDOWNOLD-MANORYOU'REGONNA-BREAKAHIP!
THAT'SSO-FUNNYIFORGOT-TOLAUGH!
ALZHEIMERS-KICKINGINALREADY-HUH?
A STICK? OH, THAT'S CREATIVE, MR. AR-TISTE.
YOU KNOW WHAT THEY SAY! STICKS AND STONES. ESPECIALLY IN YOUR CASE, GRAMPS.
OH, YEAH. FORGOT ABOUT THAT.
ALZHEIMER'S KICKING IN ALREADY, HUH?

I'D GET THAT ROCKET FUEL IF I COULD SEE WHERE IT--
KONG!

YOU KNOW IF YOU GUYS JUST ASKED POLITELY WE PROBABLY WOULD'VE GIVEN THIS TO YOU.
NANCY.
S-STOP IT! I'M S-SCARED OF THE D-DARK!
ROCKET FU

IT'S ALL TRUE. I'M J-JUST A BIG FAT BULLY!
TRUTH HURTS, DON'T IT?
GOLLY, YES!
SHRRIP!

DON'T WORRY. WE'LL FIND SOME-ONE FOR YOU TO FIGHT.
WAAAAHHH!

YOU AND YOUR BRIGHT IDEAS.
BITE ME.
REALLY PROFESSIONAL, PAT.
I LOVE YOUR ARMS.
LET'S TRADE CAPES!
I LOVE YOURS!

ALL RIGHT!!
SPACE, HERE WE COME!
STARS MY DESTINATION!!

Uh, oh.

I CAN'T BELIEVE THIS!
THIS IS WHAT WE'VE BEEN REDUCED TO? NOT ONLY THE BODIES OF CHILDREN BUT THE MINDS, TOO?
IT DOESN'T MATTER HOW OLD WE ARE, OUR HEARTS AND SOULS SHOULD STILL KNOW THE DIFFERENCES BETWEEN RIGHT AND WRONG.
WHAT HAPPENED TO UPHOLDING TRUTH, JUSTICE, AND THE AMERICAN-

WHAPP!

HEY, IT WASN'T ME! I SWEAR IT WASN'T--

WHUMPF!
HEY, I'VE GOT SOMEONE'S BLACKOUT BOMBS!!
FWAZZ!
WHACK!
THOSE AREN'T BLACKOUT BOMBS!

SEVERAL EXCRUCIATING HOURS LATER.

YOU GUYS **SUCK.**

LOZER

SO, YOU WANNA GET A LITTLE... **WET?**

IN YOUR DREAMS, "KING."

GOD, I CAN'T *WAIT* TO GET INTO SPACE.

MAN, YOUNG JUSTICE ARE GONNA BE **TICKED.**

DON'T TELL ROBIN I WAS HERE.

FWOOSH!

THERE SHE GOES.

sigh THE ***LIGHT*** OF MY LIFE.

SHE LEFT ME ***HIGH*** AND ***DRY***, KID FLASH.

THEY ***ALL*** DO, AQUABOY. THEY ALL DO.

Meanwhile...

Ah, CATWOMAN. SEEMS MY FAMILIAR, TEEKL, HAS SNIFFED YOU OUT.
BESIDES THIS BREAK-IN, I SEE, TO STEAL THE PRETTY BAUBLE, ANYTHING ELSE BRING YOU TO WASHINGTON, D.C.?
HSSS
THE SMITHSONIAN INSTITUTION
GEMSTONES of the WORLD EXHIBITION

I WAS... CURIOUS. WANTED TO SEE FOR MYSELF WHERE THE BAT WAS GOING.

CURIOSITY NORMALLY ISN'T GOOD TO FELINES...
ZAPPY
ZAPPY
HEY!

CAT'S EYE
SO LET'S PUT THE KITTY BACK IN THE CAT!

I WANT MY GEMSTONE!
FINE FOR CATWOMAN, NOT SO EASY FOR THE PINT-SIZED KITTY CAT! SHOULD I FETCH YOU A SAUCER OF MILK INSTEAD?

KLARION, YOU CHANGE ME BACK RIGHT NOW, OR...
OR WHAT, MISS "COSTUME SO BAGGY, TRIPPING OVER ANKLES"?
YOU'VE GOT ME SO, SO SCARED!
EMS of the WORLD
CAT'S EYE
PRRR
I'M NOT BEAT. NOT WHEN I CAN USE MY CAT-O'-NINE-TAILS AS A MAKESHIFT BELT!
A DOUBLE KNOT FOR EXTRA TIGHTNESS.
MARROWR!
WHOAH...
IT'S GO, KITTY, GO!
HEY, COME BACK!
Nuh-uh, PUSS 'N' BOOTS. BIGGER CATS TO FRY...
THIS IS NO PLACE FOR SOMEONE IN MY CONDITION TO BE. GOT TO FIND A WAY OUT OF HERE...
JIM ALEXANDER story
CULLY HAMNER art
COMICRAFT letters
TOM McCRAW colors
THERE HAS TO BE A CAT FLAP AROUND SOMEWHERE...
EXIT

WE'RE ON? YEAH? OKAY...
THE SCENE IS A CONFUSING ONE HERE IN WASHINGTON, AS WHAT BEGAN AS A PEACEFUL DEMONSTRATION TURNED INTO CHAOS...
HOO-BOY.
DAT DIDN'T TOIN OUT TH' WAY I FIGGERED IT WOULD, MERRY.
I T'INK I JUST MESSED T'INGS UP EVEN WORSE.
DOIBY, YOU DID FINE. NO TIME TO KICK OURSELVES OVER MIGHT-HAVE-BEENS.
DID YOU SEE WHERE ANYONE WENT IN ALL THIS MESS?
...AS A NUMBER OF YOUNG SUPER-POWERED WOULD-BE "HEROES" CLASHED WITH GOVERNMENT AGENTS ON THE GREAT LAWN MINUTES AGO.
REPORTS ARE MIXED ON WHO STARTED THE FIGHT, BUT WITNESSES AGREE THAT SUPERBOY WAS AT THE HEART OF IT.
EVERYONE, PLEASE! CLEAR THE AREA AS SAFELY AS POSSIBLE!
SOMEONE GET RID OF THESE REPORTERS!
AND WHERE DID THOSE D.E.O.☆ ASSAULT TROOPS GO?
☆DEPARTMENT OF EXTRANORMAL OPERATIONS -- Ed.
WE'VE ALSO HEARD REPORTS THAT SOME SORT OF ENERGY EFFECT WAS USED ON, OR AGAINST, A NUMBER OF THE ASSEMBLED HEROES--
--BUT ITS EFFECTS, AND WHO ORIGINATED IT, ARE NOT YET KNOWN.
Ahhhh, HELLO, CHAOS, MY OLD FRIEND...
AN ADEQUATE START, eh, TEEKL? BUT WE MUST ADD TO THE FIRE.
IF ONLY WE COULD BE EVERYWHERE AT ONCE, SO I COULD SEE HOW THOSE SUPER-DOLTS ARE COMING TO TERMS WITH WHAT'S HAPPENED TO THEM.

JLA JR. IN
YOU GOTTA BE KIDDING!
WRITTEN BY "DANNY" CURTIS JOHNSON
PENCILS BY CARLO "CARLITO" BARBERI
INKS BY WAYNE "WAYNE" FAUCHER & JUAN "TITO" VLASCO
SO... ANYONE KNOW WHY WE'RE KIDS ALL OF A SUDDEN?
NO IDEA.
HOW ABOUT ALL THOSE OTHER SUPER-PEOPLE WHO SUDDENLY SHOWED UP?
WHAT ABOUT THEM?
NO IDEA.
MAYBE THEY DIDN'T CAUSE THIS, YOU KNOW. UNTIL WE KNOW MORE ABOUT WHAT'S GOING ON, I DON'T THINK WE SHOULD BE MIXING IT UP WITH ANYONE.
YOUNG JUSTICE? ANYONE SEE WHERE THEY WENT?
NO IDEA!
ALL I CAN SAY IS, NOBODY HAD BETTER HAVE SEEN ME OUT THERE, OR ELSE.
GREAT. WELL, WHEN SOMEONE GETS A CLUE, BE SURE TO LET ME KNOW... OKAY, PEOPLE?
I SAY WE HEAD BACK OUT THERE, FIND THOSE SUPER-GOONS, AND KICK THEIR BUTTS UNTIL THEY CHANGE US BACK.
CAREFUL, MARVEL, THAT'S MY HELMET...
COLORS BY PAT "PATTY" GARRAHY
LETTERS BY DAVE "DAVY" LANPHEAR & CLEM "CLEM" ROBINS
EDITS BY MINNIE MO McTIGUE + EDDIE "el Nene" BERGANZA

YOU KNOW, IF YOU'RE WORRIED ABOUT PEOPLE SEEING YOU...
...MAYBE YOU SHOULDN'T HAVE GONE JUMPING OUT AFTER THAT WEIRD LITTLE KID.
DID THAT EVER OCCUR TO YOU?
I WAS MADE TO DO THAT BY AN OUT-SIDE FORCE, OKAY?
I THINK IT WAS DEADMAN.
Oh, THAT'S CONVENIENT. "SOMEONE ELSE MADE ME DO IT!" WHATEVER, BATS.
DON'T CALL ME "BATS," KAL.
I THINK THAT KID WAS SOME SORT OF SORCERER. THIS WHOLE THING REEKS OF MAGIC.
FOR WHATEVER REASON, HE DECIDED TO EXPLOIT THE ALREADY
DIANA! DIANA!
HANG ON A SECOND, CAP, WE NEED TO--
NO! THIS IS IMPORTANT!
THOSE PEOPLE ARE LOOKING AT US FUNNY!
THAT'S THEM! THERE THEY ARE!
IT'S THOSE KID HEROES! I SEE SUPERBOY WITH THEM!
— AND THEIR PET ROBOT!
HEY! POLICE!
ANYONE ELSE JUST HEAR A BUNCH OF MENTAL ALARM BELLS GO OFF?
THEY... THEY THINK WE'RE YOUNG JUSTICE!
BUNCHA IDIOTS.
"PET ROBOT" ...?

WHUP! TAKE COVER, PEOPLE!

SSS'EASSSY, SSSEEE? WWEEE'RE TH'JAAAAYLAAAAY AANNNNN TH'TEEENS'RE TH'DULTSS NOW!

ZZZP

ZZZP

ZZZP

ZZZP

BARTENDER, I'LL HAVE TWO OF WHATEVER HE JUST GOT!

TAKE COVER? DON'T THEY REALIZE WHO WE ARE?

KAL, WE NEED TO GET AWAY FROM HERE!

YEAH, WELL... SPEAKING OF THAT WHOLE "GETTING AWAY" THING...?
THERE'S A PROBLEM.
POINT MEN. WE'VE BEEN FLANKED.
NO WAY OUT WITHOUT GOING THROUGH SOMEONE.
GOOD!
WE DON'T WANT TO HURT ANYONE IF WE CAN HELP IT.
THESE PEOPLE ARE MISGUIDED, BUT THEY'RE JUST TRYING TO DO THEIR JOB.
OH YEAH... AND RIGHT NOW, OUR JOB IS TO TAKE YOU IN.
OKAY, BOYS, GIVE 'EM--
FOOOM
YAAH!
KOFF MY EYES... KOFF KOFF OW...
THESE FEDERAL GUYS ARE SUCH CREAM-PUFFS.
WAS SOMEONE LOOKING FOR A HANDY EXIT PATH?

LET'S JUST BE CLEAR ABOUT SOMETHING... WE DIDN'T NEED YOUR HELP, OKAY, ANARKY?
I WAS JUST ABOUT TO DO THE SAME THING.
SURE YOU WERE. CARE TO TELL US WHAT YOUR NEXT BRILLIANT IDEA IS?
YOU'RE NOT THE BOSS OF ME!
WELL, I HOPE YOU HAVE YOUR DESTINATION ALREADY FIGURED OUT.
ONCE THAT SMOKE CLEARS UP, THOSE ASSAULT TROOPS WON'T BE SHOOTING WILD ANYMORE.

YEAH, WELL... IT'S MOSTLY HERE, AND IT WOULD HAVE WORKED FINE...
...IF YOU WEREN'T TOO WORRIED ABOUT YOUR SKELETAL SYSTEM COMING ALONG WITH YOU. GOOD THING YOU DIDN'T TRY IT OUT YET.
I CAN WORK AROUND THE BUGS IN YOUR MATRIXING ROUTINE, THOUGH. IT'LL GET US THERE OKAY.
I DON'T HAVE THE ACKNOWLEDGMENT CODE TO COMPLETE THE HANDSHAKING, THOUGH.
I CAN SUPPLY THAT.
STEEL, I AM NOT GOING TO LET YOU GIVE ANARKY ACCESS TO THE WATCHTOWER.
CHILL, BATS. IT'S A ONE-TIME ENCRYPTION PAD.
IT'LL EXPIRE AFTER SIX MINUTES OF USE... JUST ENOUGH TIME FOR ALL OF US TO GET UP THERE.
DON'T CALL ME 'BATS,' JOHN.
AND, MOMENTS LATER, IN THE WATCHTOWER...
COOL. THAT'S THE LAST OF US. EVERY-ONE'S HERE.
NOW WE CAN KICK BACK AND FINALLY GET A CHANCE TO STOP RUNNING AROUND LIKE CRAZY. THAT STUN GAVE ME A KILLER HEADACHE.
KICK BACK? ARE YOU KIDDING?
HUMMM
YEAH. WE SHOULD PROBABLY GET DOWN TO THE OLD CAVE HQ WHERE EVERY-ONE'S MEETING UP.
SOMEONE GET TO THE MONITORS AND SEE WHAT THE SITUATION IS LIKE DOWN THERE.
I NEED TO GET MY ARMOR INTO THE WORKSHOP FOR A BIT, TOO.
IT'S ABOUT TEN SIZES TOO BIG RIGHT NOW.
WE CAN'T SIT AROUND HERE FOR LONG... TOO MUCH TO DO.
BUT I THINK IT'S GOOD FOR US TO CATCH OUR BREATH NOW THAT WE'RE SOMEPLACE SAFE.
WARNING.
YOU HAVE INTRUDED ON JUSTICE LEAGUE PROPERTY.
YOU WILL BE HARMLESSLY DETAINED UNTIL AN AUTHORIZED LEAGUE MEMBER ARRIVES TO DEAL WITH YOUR PRESENCE.
ON THE OTHER HAND...

EVERYBODY SCATTER! GET CLEAR!
OUR DEFENSE SYSTEM HAS GONE NUTS!
WATCHTOWER! THIS IS STEEL!
AUTHORIZE SHUTDOWN!
VOICE-PRINT MATCH IS NEGATIVE. AUTHORIZATION FAILURE.
BEING DE-AGED HAS CHANGED ALL THE BODY PARAMETERS THE TOWER USES TO IDENTIFY US--SIZE, MASS, EVEN OUR VOICES!
GOOD THING WE HAVE SOME OTHER WAY TO VERIFY, THEN!
RIGHT, PEOPLE?
WE DO HAVE SOME OTHER WAY TO SHUT THESE DOWN, RIGHT?
THERE'S MANUAL AUTHORIZATION--
BUT THE NEAREST TERMINAL IS AT LEAST A HUNDRED YARDS FROM HERE, AND THE DEFENSES WILL BE ACTIVE THE WHOLE WAY THERE.
BATMAN, CAN YOU...?
FIGURES.
YEAH, I CAN DO IT. PIECE OF CAKE.

MISTER MIRACLE HELPED US REDESIGN ALL THIS AFTER OUR LAST ENCOUNTER WITH PROMETHEUS.

THE LONGER WE RESIST THE TRAPS, THE BETTER THEY'LL GET AT ADAPTING TO US--FINDING OUR WEAKNESSES.

THE ALLOY IN THESE BANDS IS...TOUGHER THAN...THE LAST BATCH.

KZZK KZZK

I JUST NEED...A MINUTE OR SO.

...!

EEEEEE

IT'LL BE OVER, ONE WAY OR THE OTHER, IN LESS TIME THAN THAT.

SONIC BEAM, WALLY! WATCH IT! IT'LL CANCEL YOUR SUPER-SPEED VIBRATIONS!

WHOA... RINGING...

...NERVE-DARTS...NO DOUBT CARRYING SOME SORT OF FAST-ACTING MUSCLE-RELAXANT.

TING TING

THWIP

DEFENSE OVERRIDE
CALLED
AUTHORIZATION:
44510401
ACCEPTING.
TIKKATIKKATIKKATIKKA

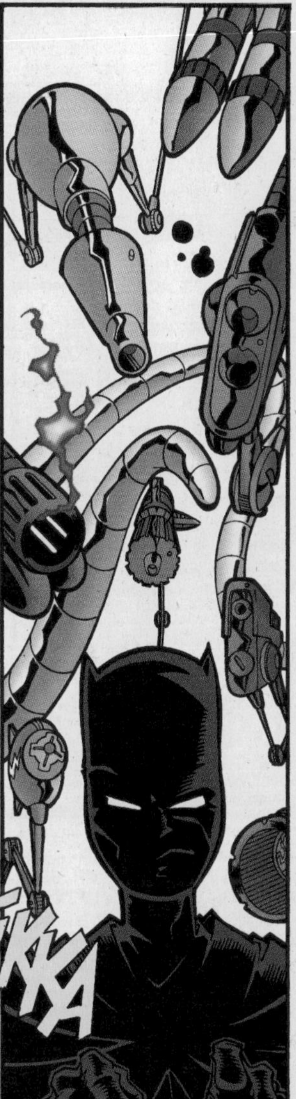

SHUTDOWN AUTHORIZED.
RIGHT.

uh-huh.
WHO'S THE BATMAN?

THAT'S A LOT BETTER. NEW METAL SUIT MAKES THE MAN.
LOOKS LIKE THINGS ARE CALMING DOWN IN WASHINGTON, AT LEAST.
...WASTING TIME...
YEAH, BUT THE MEDIA ARE MILKING THIS FOR ALL IT'S WORTH.
WAIT A SECOND-- WHAT'S THAT ONE SAYING THERE?
NEWS 7
CBTV LIVE NEWS
NEWS
WASHINGTON
BUT WHILE THE OFFICIAL STORY PAINTS A HARSH PICTURE OF THESE YOUNG WOULD-BE HEROES, PERHAPS WE SHOULD ASK OURSELVES--
HOW MUCH OF THE TRUTH ARE WE NOT HEARING?
PERHAPS THIS IS A TIME WHERE WE SHOULDN'T BE TELLING THE KIDS WHAT WE EXPECT OF THEM...
BUT RATHER LISTENING TO LEARN WHAT THEY NEED.
REPORTING FROM WASHINGTON, THIS IS ACE ATCHINSON...
SEE? IT'S NOT ALL BAD.
WE JUST NEED A FEW MORE LIKE HIM, TO SPREAD THE TRUTH.
OH, SURE. WITH MY SUPERSPEED, I COULD JUST INTERVIEW WITH EVERY REPORTER IN THE COUNTRY IN ABOUT TWO MINUTES.
WANT ME TO MAKE A FEW CALLS--SET UP A PUBLICITY TOUR?
WHAT A DUMB IDEA!
ACTUALLY, WALLY, THAT MIGHT NOT BE SUCH A BAD IDEA--GET THE WORD OUT.
BUT THERE'S NO GUARANTEE YOU'LL BE BELIEVED, SO LONG AS PEOPLE THINK ALL OF YOU ARE YOUNG JUSTICE.
IF WE CAN UNDO THIS AGING EFFECT, YOU'LL BE IN A MUCH BETTER POSITION TO HELP THE REAL KIDS.
ACCORDING TO THE MONITOR, THEY HAVEN'T REACHED THE CAVE YET. COULD BE BAD.
WE SHOULD ASSUME THESE "POINT MEN" ARE CAPABLE OF MONITORING RADIO COMMUNICATIONS, SO...
I WAS JUST ABOUT TO INITIATE A TELEPATHIC SEARCH.
THE D.E.O. CAN'T INTERCEPT PSYCHIC COMMUNICATION AS EASILY AS ELECTRONIC.

THEY'RE NOT IN WASHINGTON ANYMORE...
BUT I'VE FOUND SOME TRACES OF THE WITCH BOY...
EERIE CHILD...
HE LEAVES A STRONG PSYCHIC TRAIL IN HIS WAKE.
CAN YOU FOLLOW THE TRAIL? TRACE HIM?
LEARN ANYTHING YOU CAN ABOUT HIM?
I BELIEVE SO.
HE HASN'T GONE FAR...
AH...HERE HE COMES NOW.
AM I GOOD OR WHAT, TEEKL?
MRRROW

HEY! I'M ... I'M...
I AM!
HOW...?
YOU WOULDN'T BELIEVE HOW HARD IT IS TO RETRIEVE SOMEONE LOST IN TIME, AMAZO.
RESIDUAL SIDE EFFECT, I GUESS.
I'VE BEEN THROWING AROUND A LOT OF CHAOTIC FORCES TODAY, YES INDEED.
I DUNNO...I KINDA LIKE THIS LOOK ON YOU. MAKE THE WEAPON FIT THE CRIME!
CRIME?
YOU BETTER NOT HAVE BROUGHT ME BACK TO DO SOME PETTY...
PETTY! ARE YOU KIDDING?
I'M KLARION-- BUM BUM BUM -- THE WITCH-BOY, NOT SOME GOOFY BANK ROBBER, YOU KNOW.
I WANT YOU TO HELP ME AGAINST ALL THESE PESKY SUPER-HEROES.
OH. WELL, OKAY, THEN. THAT'S DIFFERENT.
I LIKE WALING ON SUPER-HEROES. JUST POINT THE WAY.
HMM... SPEAKING OF THE JUSTICE KIDS...
IS IT JUST ME, OR DO YOU GET THE FEELING THAT TWO'S COMPANY AND THREE'S A TERRIBLE BREACH OF SECURITY?
GOOD THING THERE ARE STILL RESIDUAL MEMORIES OF YOU TO DRAW FROM.
AND THIS --THE CAVE WHERE YOU WERE LAST DEFEATED BY HOURMAN-- MADE FOR A FINE SUMMONING LOCALE.
BUT...WHY AM I SO... YOUNG?
I'M A FREAKIN' ANDROID! I DON'T DO "YOUNG"!
AH! THERE WE GO-- I THOUGHT SO!
WHOEVER YOU ARE, YOU SEEM TO WANT TO GET A CLOSER LOOK, SO LET'S JUST PULL YOU ALL THE WAY THROUGH, SHALL WE?
GAAH!
IT'S OKAY, J'ONN. WE'RE RIGHT HERE.
YOU'RE SAFE.

I SAW HIM... THE SORCERER CHILD...
...KLARION. HE WAS...
...NO... IT'S GONE. FADED.
THIS KLARION IS THE ONE WHO DE-AGED US? AND HAS EVERYONE TURNED AGAINST US?
HE'S WORKING WITH SOME-ONE ELSE.

Aw, MAN, PLEASE! NO! A MONKEY, A CAVEMAN, A POTTED PLANT...
...MAKE ME ANYTHING BUT A TEENAGER AGAIN.
YEAH, KYLE. YOU MUST BE GOING BACK A WHOLE, WHAT, TWO OR THREE YEARS?
SHUT UP!

WELL, MAGIC MADE US THIS WAY, SO MAGIC WILL HAVE TO UNDO IT.
ANYONE GOT A SORCERER HANDY?
I KNOW A WIZARD!

A BIG WIZARD AND HE LIVES IN A CAVE AND HE'S THREE THOUSAND YEARS OLD AND EVERYTHING!
YOU BIG LIAR! YOU DO NOT KNOW A WIZARD!
WHAT'S HIS NAME, SMARTY-CAPE?
IT'S SHA...
...
I DON'T WANNA TELL YOU!

I DUNNO... SOUNDS LIKE A REAL LONG SHOT TO ME.
I SAY IT'S WORTH CHECKING OUT.
AT LEAST IT'S A START.

Oh, COME ON! WE'RE GOING OUT ON A LIMB JUST BECAUSE THE SQUIRT BABBLES ABOUT A WIZARD?
HE'D SAY HE KNEW ONE OF THOSE ELECTRIC POCKET MONSTERS IF HE THOUGHT IT WOULD GET ATTENTION!
ANYTHING IS BETTER THAN SITTING AROUND HERE.
LET'S FIND THIS WIZARD OF YOURS, CAPPIE.

HATRED... NOT OF ANY ONE PERSON OR THING, BUT RATHER AN OPEN RAGE THAT HAS NO TARGET, AND THUS, IS DIRECTED AT ALL...

"GEE, WALLY, YOU SURE DO HAVE ISSUES!"

GOLLY, OLD MAN... THANKS A LOT. YOU CAN SHUT UP NOW!

GREED... AN IMPULSE TO WANT MORE, NO MATTER HOW MUCH YOU ALREADY HAVE...
SURE, I USED TO BE A CROOK, BUT I'M NOT LIKE THAT ANYMORE.
IT NEVER EVEN CROSSES MY MIND. USUALLY... YOU KNOW.
I MEAN, IN GENERAL.
LIKE.

ENVY... THE LONGING FOR THE LIFE EXPERIENCES THAT WE WILL NEVER GET TO HAVE...
IS THIS SUPPOSED TO REPRESENT ALIENATION FROM HUMANITY? I THINK I HAVE ACCEPTED MY ROLE IN THE WORLD PRETTY WELL...
THOUGH I DO WISH I COULD BE MORE ACCEPTED AS A FATHER... AND FRIEND... SOMETIMES.

...AND PRIDE... WHICH GOETH BEFORE A FALL.
PHFYEAH, RIGHT. WE GET IT, ALREADY.
BIG LESSON TO BE LEARNED HERE, EVERY-ONE.
WHAT-EVER!

HEY, THAT'S MY WIZARD TALKING! YOU BETTER SHOW SOME RESPECT!
WHAT? YOU GONNA MAKE ME, SQUIRT?
PERHAPS HE WON'T...
...BUT MAYBE I WILL!
SEE? THAT'S MY WIZARD!

HI THERE, MISTER... um...
MY NAME... IS SHAZAM!
...MISTER SHAZAM, SIR... JUST TO FILL YOU IN ON WHAT'S HAPPENED TO US THIS AFTERNOON...
I ALREADY KNOW WHAT HAS BEFALLEN YOU.
I KNOW OF THE PLOT AGAINST YOU, AND THE WITCH-BOY WHO WARPED YOU WITH HIS CHAOS MAGIC.
THEN YOU CAN HELP US? UNDO HIS MAGIC?
I CANNOT.
THE WITCH-BOY'S SPELL WAS TANGLED TOGETHER WITH AN ARCANE SCIENCE.
THE COMBINED KNOWLEDGE OF THE QUINTESSENCE, PERHAPS, COULD UNWEAVE ITS WEB...
BUT THIS IS NOT A MATTER THAT THE QUINTESSENCE WOULD DEIGN INTERFERE WITH, I'M AFRAID.
SO THAT'S IT?
"SO SORRY, NO CAN HELP, BYE-BYE"...?
SOLOMON
HERCULES
ATLAS
ZEUS
ACHILLES
MERCURY
YOU SHALL HAVE HELP.
THE OTHERS ARE EVEN NOW ARRIVING AT YOUR CHOSEN MEETING PLACE.
YOU SHALL NEED ALL OF THEM... AS YOU SEEK SOLUTIONS... ELSEWHERE.
WELL, GREAT. NOW IT'S OFFICIAL.
THIS WAS A REALLY STUPID IDEA YOU HAD, WONDER CHICK.

IT WASN'T MY IDEA, I JUST SAID IT SOUNDED WORKABLE.
THAT'S THE SAME AS IT BEING YOUR IDEA IN THE FIRST PLACE.
IT IS NOT!
IT IS TOO!
IS NOT!
THIS IS GETTING US NOWHERE... DRAGGING THE WHOLE TEAM AROUND LIKE THIS.
I'M THROUGH RUNNING AWAY.
IS NOT! IS NOT! IS NOT! IS NOT!
ISTOO ISTOOISTOO ISTOOISTOOIS TOOISTOOIS TOOISTOO ISTOO
WHAT'S THAT SUPPOSED TO MEAN... KAL?
JUST WHAT I SAID EARLIER-- I HAVE A CITY TO WORRY ABOUT.
YOU GUYS GO AHEAD AND WASTE EVERY-ONE'S TIME.
FIND ME WHEN YOU HAVE SOME ANSWERS.
NO! DON'T GO! WE NEED EVERY-ONE!
BEAT IT, SHORT STUFF!
THE LAST THING I NEED IS YOU GETTING ALL CLINGY!
BUT... BUT...
WOW.
THIS REALLY BITES.
HE DOES HAVE A POINT, THOUGH.

DRAGGING THE WHOLE GROUP AROUND IS JUST GOING TO MAKE IT EASIER FOR OUR ENEMIES TO FIND US.
AND IT'S NOT SUCH A BAD IDEA TO CHECK UP ON THINGS BACK HOME.
WHO KNOWS WHAT ELSE THESE CONSPIRATORS HAVE GOTTEN UP TO?
GONNA SULK BACK TO GOTHAM, eh?
WHAT...WORRIED ABOUT YOUR MOMMY AND DADDY, TOO?
WHOA
THERE
CALM
DOWN
WHAT'S
YOUR
SWISH
SWISH
DAMAGE?
SPAK
SPAK
DON'T YOU EVER SPEAK TO ME ABOUT MY PARENTS, WALLY.
NOT. EVER.
NOT EVEN AFTER THIS IS ALL OVER.
DO YOU UNDER-STAND?
COOL IT! BOTH OF YOU!
YOU'RE ACTING LIKE A COUPLE OF...
...LIKE A COUPLE OF KIDS! AWWW, NUTS!
WE'RE NEVER GOING TO SOLVE THIS PROBLEM AT THIS RATE. WE'VE BEEN CRIPPLED!
I JUST... OVER-REACTED...
I'M SORRY, MAN... I'VE JUST BEEN REALLY ON EDGE SINCE THIS WHOLE THING STARTED.
WE CAN AND WE WILL SOLVE THIS PROBLEM, EVERYONE.
BUT WE'RE NOT GOING TO DO IT HERE. WE'VE GOT FRIENDS WAIT-ING FOR US ELSE-WHERE...
SO LET'S NOT WORRY THEM ANY LONGER, OKAY?

ELSEWHERE (a.k.a. THE REMAINS OF THE YOUNG JUSTICE CAVE)...

...THEN WE MADE OUR WAY HERE TO FIND THE REST OF YOU.

ASIDE FROM THE LITTLE DUST-UP OUT-SIDE*, THAT'S ABOUT IT.

SO IT'S PRETTY CLEAR THAT WE'RE GOING TO NEED TO TACKLE THIS PROBLEM FROM ALL ANGLES.

*AS SEEN IN THE SINS OF YOUTH SECRET FILES

THOUGH I WISH HE HADN'T TAKEN OFF SO IMPETUOUSLY, KAL DID HAVE A GOOD POINT.
WE NEED TO KEEP OUR ENEMIES BELIEVING THINGS ARE BUSINESS-AS-USUAL.
I'M GOING TO HEAD TO METROPOLIS TO FIND HIM BEFORE HE GETS INTO TROUBLE.
ROBIN, YOU AND BATS MIGHT WANT TO MAKE SURE GOTHAM IS OKAY.
DON'T CALL ME "BATS" KON,
WE'RE LOADIN' TH' SHIP, HEADIN' OUT T'SPACE.
IF I CAN FIX MY BUSTED ALIEN AGING GUN, MEBBE IT'LL HELP.
DIDN'T T'INK I'D BE HEADING BACK T'MYRG.
SOME OF US SHOULD GO AFTER OUR FOES DIRECTLY.
THESE POINT MEN HAVE GONE WAY TOO FAR...
I SAY WE TAKE THEM, THIS SORCERER KID, AND ANYONE ELSE WORKING WITH THEM DOWN A NOTCH OR TWO.
I'LL BE COORDINATING HERE. THE MOMENT ANYONE HAS A BREAK-THROUGH, WE'LL ALL KNOW.
NO TIME TO WAIT FOR ANY OF THE OTHERS...THE TITANS WILL HAVE TO CATCH UP LATER IF THEY CAN.
LET'S GET GOING, PEOPLE.
WE HAVE A LOT TO DO!

SINS OF YOUTH
AQUABOY & LAGOON MAN IN:
TURNING BACK THE TIDES OF TIME
SO, LADIES...
...WHO LIKES SUSHI?
BEN RAAB-writer
SUNNY LEE-penciller
LARY STUCKER & NORM RAPMUND-inkers
KEN LOPEZ-letterer
TOM McCRAW-colorist
MAUREEN McTIGUE-associate editor
EDDIE BERGANZA-editor

OOOH, I JUST LOVE IT RAW.
AND I JUST LOVE REDHEADS.
I THINK YOU AND I ARE GONNA GET ALONG JUST SWIMMING--

--LYYYY?!?

YA THINK I DON'T SEE YA MAKIN' TIME WITH MY GIRL, SQUID? I OUGHTA KICK YOUR SCRAWNY LITTLE--
UH, YOU'RE MAKING A BIG MISTAKE, FRIEND.
AM I, FISH LIPS? 'CUZ FROM THE LOOK O' IT, I'D SAY YER HEADED F'R A WORLD O' HURT...

OH, YEAH. DEFINITELY YOUR BAD...

WHAT THE HELL ARE YOU GAWKIN' AT--

--SHRIMP..?
M-M-M...
...MONSTER!!!
CLAP
I'D SAY SOMEONE'S AFRAID TO GO BACK TO THE WATER...

!
MY HERO! MMMMMM...
CALL ME, STUD. ANY TIME...
HEY, MAYBE THIS AGE-REVERSAL THING'S NOT SO BAD, AFTER ALL.

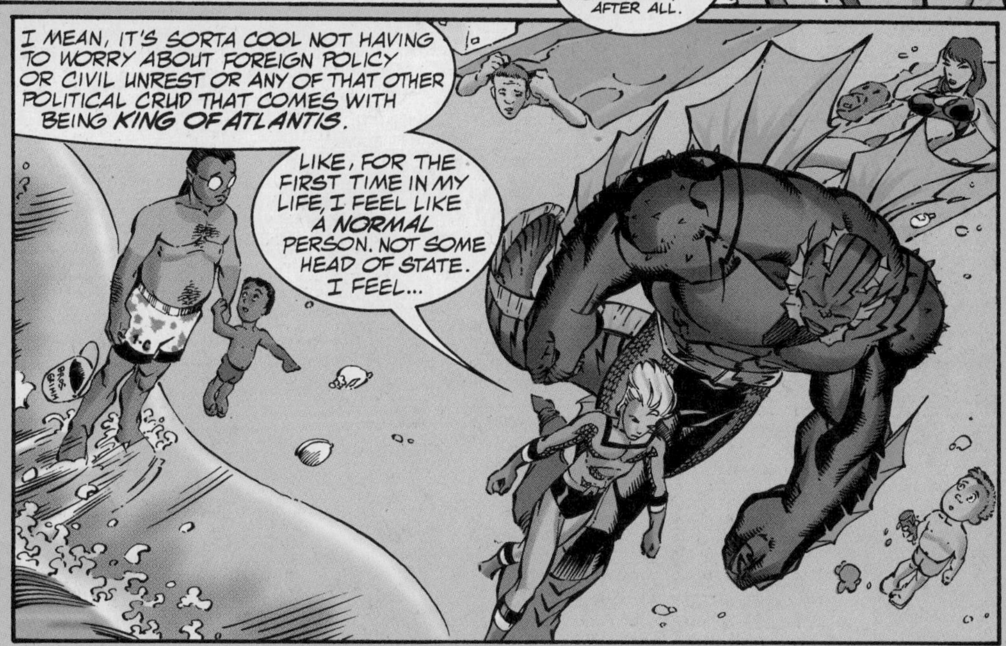
I MEAN, IT'S SORTA COOL NOT HAVING TO WORRY ABOUT FOREIGN POLICY OR CIVIL UNREST OR ANY OF THAT OTHER POLITICAL CRUD THAT COMES WITH BEING KING OF ATLANTIS.
LIKE, FOR THE FIRST TIME IN MY LIFE, I FEEL LIKE A NORMAL PERSON. NOT SOME HEAD OF STATE. I FEEL...

...COMPLETE.
TOO BAD IT CAN'T LAST.
I HEAR YA, BUDDY. FOR ME, BEING ALL GROWN UP IS LIKE, TOTAL FREEDOM.
I CAN GO WHEREVER I WANT. DO WHATEVER I WANT. AND RIGHT NOW, ALL I WANNA DO IS--
H-HELP... P-PLEASE...
UH, I WAS ACTUALLY GONNA SAY "PARTY"...

LETIFOS? WHAT ARE YOU DOING HERE?
THE CREATURES OF THE SEA TOLD ME A YOUNG ATLANTEAN HAD COME ASHORE. I EXPECTED TO FIND TEMPEST.*
I BRING DIRE TIDINGS FROM THIERNA NA OGE.
* THE "OLD" AQUALAD-- ED.
THE MYSTIC CITY? WASN'T IT DESTROYED?*
* BY THE MILLENNIUM GIANT, CERNE, IN AQUAMAN #43. --ED
THOUGH REBUILT, IT'S NOW UNDER SIEGE BY BLACK MANTA!
HE'S SEARCHING FOR RONAL'S STAFF.
UH, YOUR KINGFISHNESS? WHAT'S SHE TALKING ABOUT?
THE MOST DANGEROUS MAGICAL RELIC IN ATLANTEAN HISTORY. AN UNHOLY TALISMAN WIELDED BY A MADMAN.
ONCE A RESPECTED PHYSICIAN, RONAL OF TRITONIS WAS CORRUPTED BY THE ELDRITCH MAGICKS IMBUED WITHIN HIS HEALING STAFF. MAGICKS HE PUT TO SINISTER USE.
HIS WIFE, LORI LEMARIS, NEARLY LOST HER LIFE TO IT. IF NOT FOR THE LAST GLIMMER OF KINDNESS WITHIN HER HUSBAND, SHE WOULD HAVE DIED.
INSTEAD, SHE WAS...
...TRANSFORMED.

THAT'S IT! THAT'S WHAT WE NEED!
HEL-LOOO?!? WERE YOU LISTENING TO YOURSELF?!
WAIT, YOU'RE NOT THINKING...?
BETTER BELIEVE IT!
YOU JUST SAID THE STAFF DROVE THAT RONAL DUDE BONKOS AND YOU WANNA USE IT ON US?!?
LOOK, THIERNA NA OGE'S IN TROUBLE. AT THE VERY LEAST, I HAVE TO GO HELP THEM. IT'S MY JOB.
NOW...
...WHO WON'T FOLLOW THEIR KING?
SPLASH
BUT... BUT... THE BODACIOUS BABES!
NOW!
SPLUSH
MAN, HE CAN BE SUCH A BUZZKILL...
SPLOOSH

WHAT WERE YOU DOING IN THIERNA NA OGE, LETIFOS? I THOUGHT YOUR PEOPLE WERE ***NOMADIC***.

WE ***ARE***. AND SO SHALL WE ***REMAIN*** ONCE WE HAVE DRIVEN OFF THE EVIL GROWING AMONG OUR SETTLEMENTS.

THE DARK POWER FESTERING IN THE MYSTIC CITY SPREADS ACROSS FAIR ATLANTIS LIKE A ***CANCER***.

IT DESTROYS ***ALL*** IN ITS PATH, LEAVING ONLY ***DEATH*** IN ITS WAKE.

BEHOLD!

HOLY...

NUADA! WE'VE GOTTA GET INSIDE AND FIND HER!
WITHOUT HER MAGIC, THE CITY DOESN'T STAND A CHANCE!

EASY, KID. USE THE HEAD ON TOP OF YOUR SHOULDERS.
YOU DON'T UNDERSTAND, LAGOON BOY!
UH... THAT'S "LAGOON MAN" IN FRONT OF THE CHIQUITAS, YOUR ROYALNESS. IF YA DON'T MIND...?
"CHIQUITAS"...?

SCORE.

HEY! PLENTY OF ME TO GO AROUND, LETTY! NO NEED TO HOG THE LAGOON-STER!
UNLESS, OF COURSE, YOU LIKE TO SHARE...
GET BACK, YOU FOOL! THESE CREATURES AREN'T WHAT THEY PRETEND TO BE!
HHSSSS
HSSSS

HEY! OUCH! QUIT IT! I--I CAN'T HRR! MOVE!
WHAT THE SHELL UHNNH! ARE THEY?!?
GORGO-MAIDS.
DISTANT COUSINS OF MERMAIDS THAT DWELL IN THE SHADOWS OF DEVIL'S DEEP AND NOW SERVE THE BLACK MANTA.
PROLONGED CONTACT WITH THEIR TENTACLES INDUCES PARALYSIS, MADNESS AND EVENTUALLY, DEATH!
NOT THIS TIME!
KRAK
YOU MUSTN'T WASTE YOUR TIME FIGHTING THEM! SAVE NUADA AND DESTROY THE STAFF!
BUT--
GO! LAGOON BOY AND I--
"MAN"! LAGOON "MAN"!
--WILL HOLD OFF THESE CREATURES AND ANY OTHERS THAT DARE THREATEN OUR VICTORY!

YEAH, BUDDY. PEEP THIS ACTION, YO...
HRRRR...
OFF!
AIEEEEE!!
HOW YA LIKE ME NOW, SKANKS?
THEY WILL RETURN. WITH REINFORCEMENTS.
THEN WE'LL KICK THEIR FINS BACK TO DEVIL'S DEEP, TOO!
HOW BRAVE YOU ARE. I SEE WHY GARTH ADMIRES YOU SO.*
NOW HURRY. TIME IS SHORT...
*TEMPEST'S REAL NAME-- E.
HE IS SOMETHIN' SPECIAL, HUH?
HE IS KING...

WAM
MANTA!!!

NICE TO SEE YOU REMEMBER THE OLD ME, AQUAMAN.
OR SHOULD I SAY AQUA-BOY...?

WHY, YOU'RE THE SPITTING IMAGE OF YOUR DEAD SON...
Y-YOU'RE BACK TO NORMAL...?!?

GLORIOUS, ISN'T IT?
THOUGH I'M AFRAID THAT LOVELY SORCERESS OF YOURS DIDN'T QUITE TAKE TO HER TRANSFORMATION AS WELL AS I DID.
AS YOU CAN SEE...
NUADA!
...SHE'S IN A TERRIBLY FOUL MOOD!
SPLORCH
AGGH!
H-HEAR ME UHNH! NUADA!
YOU ARE A GAAH! A P-PRINCESS OF... THIERNA NA OGE! YOUR ARRH! WILL IS YOUR OWN!
YOUR WILL IS YOUR OWN!

HNNH... HNNH

OHHHH...

M-MY LIEGE...? IS THAT REALLY YOU...?
LONG STORY, BABE.

A TALE I IMAGINE YOU HOPED WOULD END WITH YOU IN POSSESSION OF THIS LITTLE STICK...
GIVE ME THE STAFF, MANTA. YOU'VE CAUSED ENOUGH TROUBLE WITH IT ALREADY.

YOU THINK YOU CAN TAKE IT FROM ME, LITTLE BOY?
COME AND GET IT!!!

WHAT THE HALIBUT'S TAKING HIM SO LONG?
WHOOSH
YOU DON'T THINK MANTA'S BEATEN HIM, DO YOU?
WHOOMP
HAVE FAITH, LAGOON BOY.
F'R THE UMPTEENTH TIME, IT'S LAGOON "MAN"!
AWWW, SHELL, I GIVE UP...
HE WILL NOT FAIL...

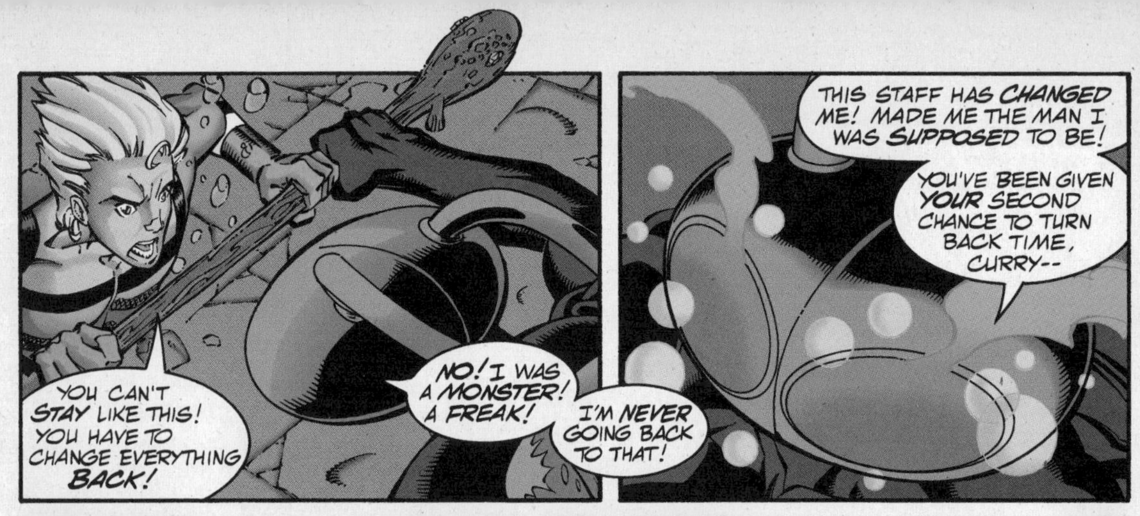
YOU CAN'T STAY LIKE THIS! YOU HAVE TO CHANGE EVERYTHING BACK!
NO! I WAS A MONSTER! A FREAK!
I'M NEVER GOING BACK TO THAT!
THIS STAFF HAS CHANGED ME! MADE ME THE MAN I WAS SUPPOSED TO BE!
YOU'VE BEEN GIVEN YOUR SECOND CHANCE TO TURN BACK TIME, CURRY--
--NOW I WANT MINE!
ZZAAAZT
YOU'RE WRONG, MANTA. YOU ALREADY HAD YOUR SECOND CHANCE, AND YOU BLEW IT BY SELLING YOUR SOUL TO NERON!
WE ARE WHO WE ARE. NOTHING CAN CHANGE THAT.
NOT A HOOK FOR A HAND. NOT LONG HAIR OR A BEARD. NOT BEING A TEENAGER OR AN ADULT.
NONE OF THAT STUFF MATTERS BECAUSE IN THE FINAL ANALYSIS I AM STILL KING OF ATLANTIS--

--AND MY WILL BE DONE!
FZLASH
NO!!!
WITHOUT THE STAFF, I CANNOT REMAIN--
--HUMANNNN...

WE ARE WHO WE ARE...
MAGNIFICENT, ISN'T IT?
NEVER FELT ANYTHING LIKE IT BEFORE. IT'S AWESOME...
THE STAFF CAN TURN YOU BACK THE WAY YOU WERE. MAKE YOU WHOLE AGAIN.
CAN IT RESTORE THIERNA NA OGE AND THE REST OF MANTA'S DAMAGE?
YES... BUT BEWARE.
YOU MAY USE THE STAFF BUT ONCE, LEST YOU RISK DAMNING NOT ONLY YOUR OWN MORTAL SOUL...
...BUT ALSO THOSE OF EVERY LIVING CREATURE WITHIN YOUR KINGDOM.
JEEZ... HAVE SOME PRESSURE...

ARE YOU CERTAIN ABOUT THIS, SIRE? THIS IS YOUR CHANCE TO UNDO ALL THE DAMAGE THAT'S EVER BEEN DONE TO YOU.
A CHANCE TO BEGIN ANEW...
I...
NO. MY PEOPLE COME FIRST, NUADA.
THEN LET US BEGIN...
HRRRR...
AAAH!

WOW.
CRIK
CRAK
CRUUMBLE
CRASH

UHNNH!
OHHH!
QUICKLY! WE MUST FIND A HEALER!
EASY, CHAMP. I'VE GOT YA.
WAIT! THERE'S SOMETHING I'VE GOTTA DO FIRST...

...
"HEAVY IS THE HEAD THAT WEARS THE CROWN."
SNAP
YOU MADE A WISE DECISION, SIRE. THANKS TO YOU, ALL ATLANTIS SHALL LIVE AGAIN.
SURELY THERE MUST BE SOME REWARD I CAN BESTOW UPON YOU FOR YOUR BRAVERY...?
NUDGE NUDGE
OH, YOU LUCKY DAWGFISH!
IF ONLY YOU COULD TURN BACK THE TIDES OF TIME...

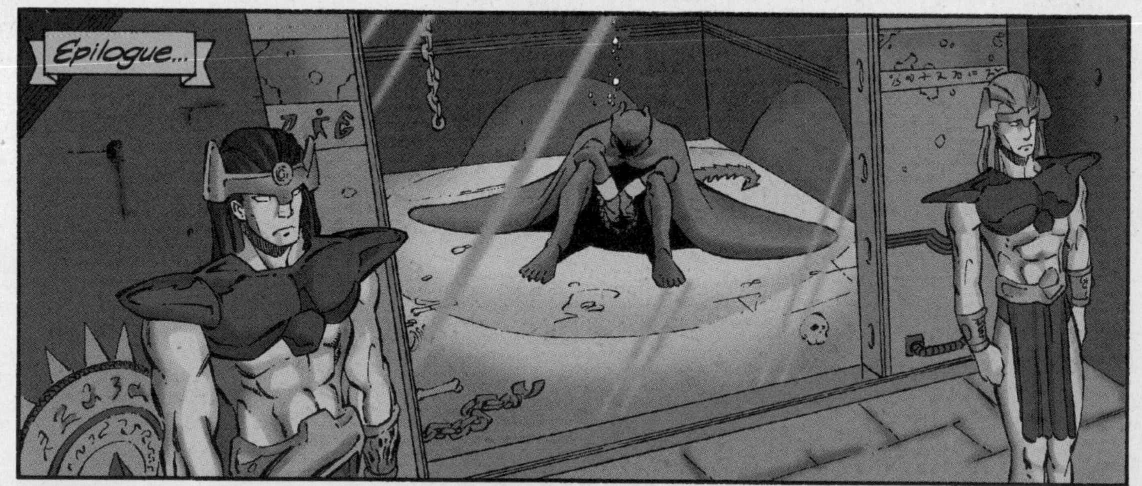

YOU'RE IN LUCK, MR. MANTA--
--BECAUSE I HAVE JUST THE THING FOR YOU!
MMRROWWW.

WASHINGTON, D.C.

THE SMITHSONIAN NATIONAL MUSEUM OF NATURAL HISTORY.

THIS SUCKS.

NOT FOR ME. *I* LIKE THE CHANGE.

WE'RE ALMOST THERE... JUST HOLD ON TIGHT.

"Wisdom, Like Age..."

SCOTT BEATTY WRITER SUNNY LEE PENCILS NORM RAPMUND INKS COMICRAFT LETTERS TOM McCRAW COLORS

WHAT MAKES YOU THINK KLARION WAS REALLY HERE, MARY?

YOU'RE KIDDING, RIGHT?

THIS HAS *WITCH BOY* WRITTEN ALL OVER IT.

LISTEN, FREDDY... AFTER WHAT HAPPENED TO ALL US HEROES, I THINK YOU SHOULD SIT THIS ONE OUT.

IS *THAT* WHAT BEING AN ADULT FEELS LIKE?

YOU GET ALL WORRISOME AND ANXIOUS OF IMPENDING DOOM.

I'M SERIOUS.

NO WAY. *uh-uh*...

CAPTAIN NAZI!
KLARION!
BUM... BUM... BUM..! THE WITCH BOY!
SAY IT RIGHT OR DON'T SAY IT AT ALL!
KNEEL BEFORE THE NEW HITLER YOUTH.
OOP. GOTTA GO.
UHN!
NOTHING WILL STOP ME FROM RESURRECTING MY FÜHRER AND ERECTING A NEW MILLENNIAL REICH!
RAISING THE DEAD IS SO LAST YEAR'S CRISIS, SHORTY.
SCHWEIN MARVELS!
MARY! THE KIDS!
P-TOING
GOTCHA!
VERE IST YOUR STRENGTH OF HERCULES?
VERE IST YOUR SPEED OF MERCURY?
VERE IST YOUR WISDOM OF SOLOMON?

FREDDY!
HAH! YOU ARE NOTHING!
YEAH?
JA!
I'M CAPTAIN MARVEL JR., YOU NAZI JERK.
ZZZAAAAKK
WHO SAYS KLARION STOLE YOUR THUNDER?
VERY FUNNY. LET'S JUST FIND THE PASTY LITTLE WARLOCK AND SET THINGS RIGHT...
I'M NOT SURE I'M READY FOR A MAY-DECEMBER ROMANCE.
ach.
IN YOUR DREAMS. LITTLE BOY...
...IN YOUR DREAMS.
END

I'M NOT SURE I CAN DO THIS...
YOU HAVE TO. NOW STOP WORRYING AND MOVE.
uh-uh. ALL RIGHT. I GUESS.

BATBOY AND ROBIN IN Big Magic

WOW, THIS THING LOOKS LIKE THE COCKPIT OF THE CONCORDE.
I'LL GUIDE YOU THROUGH.
DOES THIS COSTUME ALWAYS FIT THIS TIGHT?
YOU WERE A BIGGER KID THAN ME.
LOOK ON THE BRIGHT SIDE, BRUCE...
... AT LEAST THE SHORT-SHORTS AREN'T PART OF THE OUTFIT ANYMORE.
GODSPEED, GENTLEMEN...
AND I HOPE NO ONE MINDS IF I HAVE A BIT OF A LIE-DOWN.

HOW ARE YOU DOING?
NOT BAD.
IT MIGHT BE WORTH TWENTY YEARS OFF MY LIFE TO HAVE THE KEYS TO THIS.
FEEL THAT POWER.
YOU'VE BEEN IN IT BEFORE.
BUT NOT BEHIND THE WHEEL.
UNLESS WE FIND KLARION, YOU MAY HAVE A CHANCE TO GET USED TO IT.
ANY IDEAS?
KLARION HAS USED GOTHAM AS A BASE OF OPERATIONS BEFORE...
...AND I KNOW SOMEONE WHO MIGHT BE ABLE TO HELP US FIND HIM.
HEAD FOR MIDTOWN...
ZATANNA

"... I ONLY HOPE I CAN CONVINCE HER TO *HELP* US."
YOU?!
IT IS OF UTMOST *URGENCY* TO THE PERSONS I'M REPRESENTING.
SO'S MY *CAREER* TO ME.
MAYBE YOU WAIT UNTIL MY *SHOW* IS OVER, AND--
I AM FEARFUL THAT *TIME* IS A LUXURY WE CANNOT AFFORD.
I'M NOT GOING *ANY*WHERE WITH YOU.
YOU *WILL* COME.
FIVE *MINUTES*, MISS ZATANNA!
I'M NOT SURE I HAVE *THAT* LONG.

SGUB OT STELLUB!
UNNH?
I HEARD YOUR POWERS WERE CONSIDERABLE.
GAAH!
BUT THEY ARE MERE TRICKS.
Uhhh!
CHILD'S PLAY.
KRRK
UNNGH!
SSSHHH!
TAKE HER WITH US! HURRY!
THE BROTHERS ARE WAITING!

LOOKS LIKE THE MAGICIAN DISAPPEARED, MONTOYA.
AND LEFT A MESS BEHIND, HARV.
HELLUVA STRUGGLE. GUESS WE CAN RULE OUT STAGE FRIGHT.
NO BLOOD, NO SHOTS FIRED.
I'M THINKING ABDUCTION.
THEN IT'S NOT A CLEAR HOMICIDE?
WHAT BRINGS YOU DOWN HERE, COMMISH?
THIS HAS THE POTENTIAL TO BE A HIGH-PROFILE CASE.
I COULD WRITE THE LEAD MYSELF-- "WORLD-FAMOUS ENTERTAINER KIDNAPPED."
CRIME SCENE'S HERE. WE'LL GET SOMETHING.
NO REASON TO THINK ZATANNA IS DEAD.
CRIME SCENE
POLICE LINE
CHICK LIKE HER, GOTTA BE A RANSOM DEAL.
KEEP ME POSTED.
ANYTHING YOU NEED, YOU'VE GOT IT.

CRIM
SCEN
GOTHAM
BWOOP-
BWOOP
DID I HEAR THE SCANNERS RIGHT?
Uh...?
DEPENDS ON WHAT YOU *HEARD.*
ZATANNA IS *GONE.*
THE *OFFICIAL* STORY IS THAT SHE'S ILL AND CANCELED HER PERFORMANCE.

I CAN READ BETWEEN THE LINES, COMMISSIONER.
THAT'S A LITTLE FORMAL, ISN'T IT?
"JIM." I CALL HIM "JIM."
Uh... JIM. COMMISSIONER JIM.
ANY LEADS?
ARE YOU... ALL RIGHT?
Um... SURE. NEVER BEEN BETTER.
YOU HAVEN'T PULLED ANOTHER SWITCH ON ME, HAVE YOU?
TELL HIM YOU PROMISED THAT WOULD NEVER HAPPEN AGAIN.
I TOLD YOU THAT WOULD NEVER HAPPEN AGAIN.
FORGET IT.
I'LL GIVE YOU WHAT WE HAVE, AND IT'S NOT MUCH.

no... no...
...away from me... away...
I HAVE HOLD OF YOUR MIND, ZATANNA...
YOUR EVERY THOUGHT IS MINE...
ENOUGH OF THIS, GREGOR.
RELEASE HER!
THE FEAR GROWS IN HER.
SHE WILL DO AS WE SAY. DO... ANYTHING WE SAY.

WE SAID ENOUGH, GREGOR!
WHAT USE IS SHE TO US IF YOU DESTROY HER BRAIN?
NIKO, VANI... HER WILL IS STRONG ZATANNA MUST BE BROKEN...
WE NEED HER STRONG!
SHE MUST UNDO THE CURSE PLACED ON US...
... BY THAT ROMANI WITCH!
ZATANNA'S POWERS ARE LEGENDARY!
ONLY SHE CAN MAKE US TWO FROM ONE!

ICEBERG LOUNGE
IS THERE A PROBLEM HERE?
THERE CERTAINLY IS.
I DON'T MIND SKIRTING THE LAW NOW AND THEN--
-- BUT I'M NOT GETTING SHUT DOWN BECAUSE SOME KID WANTS TO DRINK A MAI-TAI.
BUT I'M VERY MATURE FOR MY YEARS.
LISTEN, KID. GET YOUR PRE-PUBESCENT BUTT OUT ON THE STREET, OR YOU'LL GO HOME TO MAMA WITH A BROKEN ARM.
THAT'S BARELY HOSPITABLE.
AND I FIND YOU... TIRESOME.
Whaaaaa?!
NOW WHO'S UNDERAGE?

КТО ЭТО?
THE *BAT*?

I HAVE A FEW *QUESTIONS* FOR YOU, SERGEI.
AND I *DON'T* APPRECIATE BEING SHOT AT BY YOUR *VORY*.

YOU'RE TALKING TOO MUCH.
LIGHTEN UP.

A KIDNAPPING.
A MAGICIAN.
I KNOW NOTHING OF THIS.
YOU'RE LYING.
...
MAGIC?
YOU WANT THE TWINS.
TWINS?
NIKO AND VANI ASALACHI. CHECHIANS.
SPELLS AND WITCHES AND ALL OF THAT NONSENSE.
THEY HAVE AN IMPORTS WAREHOUSE ON BILLINGS.
YOU DID VERY WELL.
IT'S EASY. YOU DO SCARE PEOPLE.
FEAR IS OUR WEAPON.

FUNNY THING...
... I NEVER THOUGHT ABOUT DOING THIS.
THOUGHT ABOUT DOING WHAT?
WEARING THIS OUTFIT. BEING YOU. BEING BATMAN.
YOU DON'T LIKE IT?
IT'S COOL, BUT IT'S NOT ME.
MAYBE IT WILL BE SOMEDAY. BUT I DON'T THINK SO.
I NEVER REALLY THOUGHT ABOUT A LEGACY. I THOUGHT ONE NIGHT I MIGHT BE JUST A FRACTION OF A SECOND TOO SLOW, AND--
BUT WHAT HAPPENS AFTER THAT?
I'LL STILL BE HERE TO FIGHT THE GOOD FIGHT, BRUCE.
THAT'S GOOD TO KNOW.
I'M JUST NOT SURE...
... I'D WANT IT TO BE AS BATMAN.

I CANNOT DO THIS.
YOU DON'T KNOW WHO I AM.
I AM WHITE MAGIC... NOT THE DARK ARTS.
THE PREPARATIONS HAVE BEEN MADE, ZATANNA.
IT IS ONLY THE POWER OF YOUR MAGIC THAT WE NEED.
UP
I CANNOT DO THIS...
... TO USE THE DARK SORCERIES... IS TO BECOME THEM.
DO THIS OR LOSE YOUR MIND!
DO THIS OR WRESTLE WITH THE DEMONS WITHIN YOUR SKULL FOR AN ETERNITY!
DO NOT DEFY ME.
THE AGONIES... THE UGLINESS I HAVE PLACED THERE IS BUT A TASTE OF THE FATE THAT MAY AWAIT YOU.

BAAAAAASSSSH!
GAAAH!
RESCUE ZATANNA, I'LL TAKE THE TWINS.
ARE YOU... *SURE?* THEY'RE *HUGE.*
SIZE IS NOT A *FACTOR.* PHYSICAL MEMORY IS MORE IMPORTANT.
BUT...
DO AS I *SAY*...
TRUST ME!
OKAY...
FRIENDS OF YOURS, eh?
I WONDER HOW STRONG THE MIND OF THE *BATMAN* IS?
NO...

KILL HIM!
UGH!
I WILL FIND HIS THOUGHTS... TURN THEM AGAINST HIM...
CATCH HIM!
HE IS SO *FAST!*
Ahh... A STRONG MIND... VERY INTENSE...
...BUT THERE IS *SORROW* THERE...
WUFF!
UNFF!

SOMETHING IN THE PAST... A TRAGEDY...
uh?
MY GOD...
MOTHER... FATHER...
henh...
YOU HAVE NOT AVENGED US.
OUR KILLER IS STILL FREE.
NO...
I'VE TRIED... I'VE DONE NOTHING ELSE...
HAH!
WHAT IS GOING ON?!
HOW DO YOU WITHSTAND MY PSYCHIC ASSAULT?!
I DON'T WANT TO TELL YOU YOUR BUSINESS, SHORTY...

ARRRHH!
... BUT MAYBE YOU HAVE THE WRONG BATMAN.
EKANS OT REGGAD!
HSSSSSS
ZATANNA, ARE YOU ALL RIGHT?
HOW DID YOU...?
HELP YOUR MENTOR...
HE NEEDS YOU...
YAAAAHH!!!
uh...?
KRSSH!

NOOOOOOOO
UP
TURNS OUT HE DIDN'T NEED ME.
I TOLD YOU. IT'S A MATTER OF PHYSICAL MEMORY.
AND SPEAKING OF THINGS PHYSICAL...
NAM OT YOB DNA YOB OT NAM EGNAHC!
I CAN'T. THE WITCHBOY'S MAGIC IS TOO POWERFUL.
I'M AFRAID TO TRY AGAIN. THE NEXT CHANGE MAY BE MORE DIRE...

IT WAS WORTH A SHOT.
... THAN A CHANGE IN WARDROBE.
WHAT WILL YOU DO?
GET BACK WITH THE OTHERS WHO'VE BEEN ALTERED.
BUT THE JLA ARE ALL TEENAGERS NOW. THEIR JUDGMENT'S WAY OFF.
YOU WERE BORN A GROWNUP.
THEN THE FATE OF THE WORLD IS IN THE HANDS OF YOUNG JUSTICE.
NOT GOOD.
DROP YOU SOMEWHERE, ZATANNA?
I'D BETTER STAY AND EXPLAIN THINGS.
SORRY I COULDN'T BE MORE HELP.
HAVE TO SAY I LEARNED A LOT TONIGHT...
... FROM DRIVING THE CAR TO A FEW THINGS ABOUT MYSELF.
SO DID I, TIM.
SO DID I.
SINS OF YOUTH

MEDIA BLITZ
I FEEL LIKE RUNNING, SO I DO. USUALLY IT MAKES ME FEEL BETTER. NOT TODAY.
TODAY I CAN'T FIND MY RHYTHM. MY CONCENTRATION IS SHOT. MY BLOOD IS AWASH WITH HORMONES.
MY PULSE SURGES, APPROACHING TACHYCARDIA.
I'M AWKWARD, CLUMSY... SLOW.
WHEN I SAY "SLOW," I'M SPEAKING RELATIVELY, OF COURSE.
MY NAME IS WALLY WEST. I'M KID FLASH
DWAYNE McDUFFIE
WRITER
ANGEL UNZUETA
PENCILLER
JAIME MENDOZA
INKER
CHRIS ELIOPOULOS
LETTERER
MOOSE BAUMANN
COLORS/SEPS
MIKE McAVENNIE &
L.A. WILLIAMS
EDITORS
IMPULSE
CREATED BY
MARK WAID &
MIKE WIERINGO

EVER HAVE ONE OF THOSE DAYS?
IT STARTS OUT TYPICALLY ENOUGH -- YOU TEAM UP WITH AN ASSEMBLAGE OF THE MOST POWERFUL BEINGS ON THE FACE OF THE EARTH AND STRIVE TOGETHER TO MAKE THE WORLD SAFE FOR...
...WELL, TEENAGERS. YOUNG JUSTICE, IN THIS PARTICULAR CASE. LET'S TRY NOT TO GET BOGGED DOWN IN DETAILS.
WHAT'S IMPORTANT IS WHAT HAPPENS NEXT. ONE SECOND YOU'RE AN ADULT -- IN MY CASE, THE FLASH, FASTEST MAN ALIVE --
-- THE NEXT, YOU'RE SOMEHOW SUDDENLY 13 YEARS OLD. WHICH WASN'T EVEN THAT MUCH FUN THE FIRST TIME AROUND.
AND JUST WHEN YOU THINK THINGS COULDN'T POSSIBLY GET ANY WORSE...
WALLY!

...YOU DISCOVER YOU'RE NOT THE ONLY ONE WHOSE AGE HAS BEEN ADJUSTED.
WALLY, DON'T YOU HEAR ME? WAIT UP A SECOND!
THAT'S THE KIND OF DAY I'M TALKING ABOUT.
YOU'RE THE GROWNUP NOW, IMPULSE. I'M SURE YOU CAN KEEP UP.
NOT THE POINT. WE'RE SUPPOSED TO BE WORKING TOGETHER, AND YOU RUN OFF WITH NO EXPLANATION. I'VE BEEN CHASING YOU FOR NEARLY THREE-HUNDRED MILES.
NO DISCUSSION NO PLAN, NO NOTHING. DON'T YOU THINK YOU'RE BEING JUST A LITTLE IMPULSIVE HERE?
I'LL DEFER TO YOUR LEGENDARY EXPERTISE IN THIS AREA.
BOY, ANYBODY EVER TELL YOU THAT YOU'RE A REAL SURLY KID?
NOT FOR YEARS, THANKS.
SO, YOU WANT TO TELL ME WHERE WE'RE GOING?
"WE" AREN'T GOING ANYWHERE. I'M GOING TO SEE MY WIFE. OR DID YOU FORGET I'M SUPPOSED TO BE ON MY HONEYMOON?

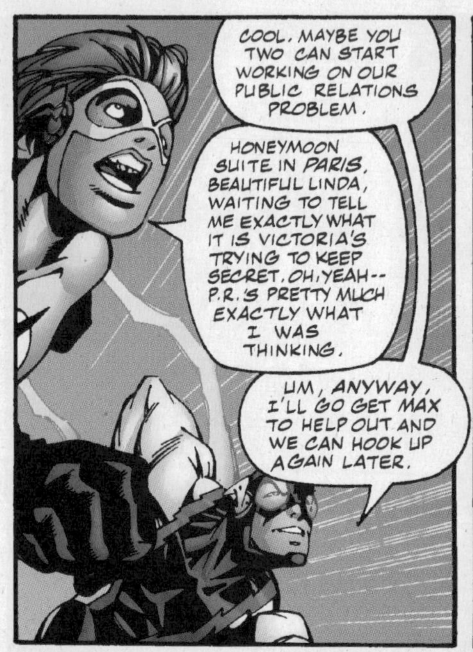

MANCHESTER, ALABAMA...

...CONTINUES WITH OUR SPECIAL COVERAGE: "JUNIOR JLA OR SUPER-JUVENILE DELINQUENTS?" YOU'RE WATCHING THE RUPERT NEWS CHANNEL. "WE PURPORT, YOU DECIDE."

THEY'RE SUPPOSED TO BE HEROES IN TRAINING, THE NEXT GENERATION JUSTICE LEAGUE. BUT ARE THEY REALLY OFFERING US A HELPING HAND? OR ARE THEY ACTUALLY DANGEROUS JUVENILE DELINQUENTS?

THIS IS BAD...

WE TALKED TO A JOURNALIST WHO COVERS THE METAHUMAN BEAT...
THIS IS EXACTLY WHAT HAPPENS WHEN LIBERAL SOCIAL POLICY...
MAX?
HAVE YOU BEEN FOLLOWING THIS? IT'S ON EVERY CHANNEL.
UH, YEAH, MAX, ACTUALLY, I'M KINDA INVOLVED.
BIG SURPRISE THERE.
YOU SOUND ODD. IS YOUR VOICE STARTING TO CHANGE?
AMONG OTHER THINGS.
BART?!
YEAH, IT'S ME.
WHAT HAPPENED? ARE YOU TIME-TRAVELING?
I WISH. NO, ME AND SOME OF THE GUYS...
...WE HAD A LITTLE ACCIDENT.
I WOULD...
MAYBE I BETTER SIT DOWN.

PARIS, FRANCE...

LINDA? I'M BACK!
ABOUT TIME YOU GOT HERE, MISTER. IT'S RUDE TO KEEP DUCKING OUT ON YOUR HONEYMOON, EVEN IF YOU ARE OUT SAVING THE WORLD.
ANYWAY, COME HERE. I'VE GOT A SURPRISE FOR YOU.

ME, TOO...
...AND I THINK I'D BETTER GO FIRST...

MANCHESTER, ALABAMA...
THAT'S ONE HELL OF A MESS, BART--

--ALL OF YOUNG JUSTICE ARE TRAPPED IN THE BODIES OF ADULTS?
AND MOST OF THE ADULT SUPER-HEROES HAVE BEEN TURNED INTO TEENAGERS?
EXCEPT FOR SUPERBOY, AT FIRST. HE'S ALWAYS GOTTA BE DIFFERENT.

LET ME PUT IT THIS WAY: BY NOW THERE MUST BE A DOZEN COPIES OF THE LATEST HARD KORE CD IN THE JLA WATCHTOWER.
BUT YOU KNOW THOSE GUYS. SOMEBODY'LL FIGURE OUT HOW TO PUT THINGS RIGHT, SOONER OR LATER.

IN THE MEANTIME, WE'VE GOT A JOB TO DO, SO SUIT UP. WITH MAX MERCURY HELPING US, THE PRESS'LL HAVE TO BELIEVE OUR STORY. I MEAN, WHAT WITH YOUR ELDER STATESMAN STATUS AND ALL.
THAT'S A GOOD PLAN, BART, AND EXTREMELY WELL THOUGHT-OUT...
IT HAPPENS SOMETIMES. LAW OF AVERAGES.
...BUT I CAN'T HELP YOU ON THIS ONE. I--I HAVE REASONS WHY I CAN'T BE PART OF ANY PRESS TOUR.*
OH. WELL, DON'T WORRY ABOUT IT, MAX. IT'S MY RESPONSIBILITY. I'LL HANDLE IT.
LOOKING AT YOU RIGHT NOW, I HAVE NO DOUBT YOU WILL. I ALWAYS KNEW YOU'D LIVE UP TO BARRY ALLEN'S LEGACY.
*SEE CURRENT ISSUES OF IMPULSE FOR DETAILS.
I MIGHT GOOF AROUND A LOT, MAX, BUT I'VE ALWAYS UNDERSTOOD WHAT I'M TRAINING FOR.
THE WORLD NEEDS HEROES. IT NEEDS THE FLASH.
LOOKS LIKE I'M YOUR MAN.
I BETTER GET GOING. BUT MAX?
IF YOU EVER DECIDE YOU WANT TO LET ME IN ON WHATEVER IT IS YOU'RE HIDING, I'M HERE FOR YOU.
GODSPEED, SON.
THANKS, BUT I'M GOING TO TRY KEEPING IT JUST UNDER GODSPEED.

--I SEE WHAT YOU MEAN, WALLY. IT REALLY IS A SPIN CONTROL PROBLEM.
MAYBE YOU COULD DO A PIECE ABOUT IT, GET THE TRUE STORY OUT THERE.
THAT'S NOT GOING TO FLY, HONEY. EVERYBODY KNOWS I'M MARRIED TO THE FLASH. MY OBJECTIVITY WOULD BE COMPROMISED.
WELL, WE WOULDN'T WANT YOU COMPROMISED.
I COULD ASK FRAN BECKER TO DO A PIECE. SHE OWES ME A FAVOR OR TWO.
WHAT YOU REALLY NEED IS A MEDIA CONSULTANT. I KNOW A GUY WHO DOES IT FOR REGIS. HE USED TO WORK FOR BOOSTER GOLD, SO HE KNOWS METAHUMAN--
--STUFF...
WHAT?
IT IS OUR Honeymoon.
YOU GOTTA BE KIDDING.

SORRY, HOT PANTS. UNTIL YOU'RE OLD ENOUGH TO SHAVE AGAIN, THIS IS A TOTALLY PLATONIC HONEYMOON.

YOU'RE RIGHT. I DON'T KNOW WHAT'S THE MATTER WITH ME. I'VE GOT TO KEEP IT UNDER CONTROL.
IT'S PROBABLY ALL THE NEW HORMONES HITTING YOU AT ONCE. IS IT THIS BAD FOR THE OTHER JLAers?
JUST BE THANKFUL YOU'RE NOT MARRIED TO AQUAMAN.

WALLY, COME HERE.

I'M THANKFUL THAT I'M MARRIED TO YOU.
DO NOT DISTURB

DON'T WORRY, IT'S GOING TO BE OKAY. WE'LL GET THROUGH THIS TOGETHER.
OKAY, YOU GOTTA GET GOING. SCOOT.
HUH? OH, RIGHT.

WAYNE-TECH
CHIANG RESTAURANT COCKTAILS
DELI
PARK LOCK
AND SHORTLY...
THERE YOU ARE! SAY, DID YOU EVER NOTICE HOW MUCH BIGGER I AM AS AN ADULT THAN YOU WERE?
THAT WAS DOWNRIGHT INFANTILE, BART.
SHOOT. MAX WAS JUST TELLING ME HOW MATURE I'VE BEEN ACTING ALL DAY.
HE'S PROBABLY JUST REACTING TO YOUR NEW LOOK.
YEAH, SPEAKING OF CLOTHES, WHAT'S WITH YOUR GOOFY OUTFIT? WHY NOT USE THE SPEED FORCE TO CHANGE IT BACK?
"GOOFY"? MY KID FLASH COSTUME IS ONE OF THE ALL-TIME CLASSICALLY COOL SUPER-SUITS!
THAT YELLOW ONE, WITH THE PETER PAN BOOTIES?
ROBIN WORE THE BOOTIES. ANYWAY, IF IT WEREN'T FOR MY RESPECT FOR BARRY'S* LEGACY, I'D WEAR THIS ALL THE TIME.
THE ONE YOU'VE GOT ON NOW?
*BARRY WAS WALLY'S MENTOR AND BART'S GRANDFATHER.
I FIGURE UNTIL THIS IS SORTED OUT, THERE'S NO REASON NOT TO INDULGE IN A LITTLE NOSTALGIA.
'CAUSE I'VE GOT NO PROBLEM WITH YOU WEARING MY OLD IMPULSE COSTUME FOR A WHILE. THEN WE'D MATCH.
FORGET IT, BART.
NO, REALLY. THINK ABOUT IT...
BLÜDHAVEN 4 MI
OPAL CITY 180 MI
L.A. 1969 MI
IMPULSE AND KID IMPULSE!
HEY! YOU DON'T CALL ME "KID."
SURE THING. UM, WHERE ARE WE GOING?

... AND LATER ON "WATCH OUT!", WE'LL TALK ABOUT THOSE BRATTY SUPER KIDS WHO HAVE THE HILL IN AN UPROAR...
WLAN
KLIK
... SHUT UP! SHUT UP! THERE IT IS ON TAPE! THE JUNIOR JLA BLEW UP MOUNT RUSHMORE! THIS IS CHRIS MATTHEWS! SHUT UP!
KLIK
...SLUDGE REPORT ALSO HAS AN EXCLUSIVE RUMOR ABOUT ALLEGED MISCONDUCT BETWEEN SUPERMAN AND WONDER WOMAN. NOW THAT I'VE SAID IT ON TV, IT'S NEWS!
KLIK
... JUNIOR JUSTICE LEAGUE CAUSED THE EXPLOSION THAT DEFACED MOUNT RUSHMORE, ONLY DAYS BEFORE GETTING INTO A BRAWL ON THE WHITE HOUSE LAWN. I'M NINA JUSTIS.
KLIK
IT'S LIKE THAT ON EVERY CHANNEL. I GOTTA SAY, YOU GUYS PRESENT A REAL CHALLENGE.
BUT TED BARTON, MEDIA CONSULTANT EXTRAORDINAIRE, LOVES A CHALLENGE.
TED BARTON ALSO APPARENTLY LIKES TALKING ABOUT HIMSELF IN THE THIRD PERSON.
A SENSE OF HUMOR! GOOD. YOU'RE GOING TO NEED IT.
TED BARTON HAS A PLAN TO COUNTER YOUR MASSIVE NEGATIVE SPIN, DESPITE THE FACT THAT TED BARTON THINKS YOU PROBABLY DESERVE IT.
TED BARTON LIKES MOUNT RUSHMORE. TED BARTON ISN'T TOO DIFFERENT FROM MOST AMERICANS.
TED BARTON FEARS METAHUMANS, BUT IS SECRETLY ASHAMED AT OWING YOU SO MUCH.
TED BARTON WONDERS WHY SO MANY OF YOU WEAR YOUR UNDERPANTS ON THE OUTSIDE OF YOUR CLOTHES.

YOU EVER BEEN THREE FEET FROM DARKSEID? WE WEAR THEM ON THE OUTSIDE SO WE DON'T SOIL THEM.
YOU'RE GOING TO WORK OUT NICELY. WISH TED HAD TIME TO BOOK YOU ON LENO.
LETTERMAN'S FUNNIER.
CONAN'S FUNNIER THAN BOTH OF THEM.
YOU'RE AWAKE AT 12:30?
UM... SOMETIMES.
PLEASE DON'T TELL MAX.
HERE'S WHAT WE'RE GOING TO DO: A LITTLE SUPER-SPEED STUNT TO DRAW ATTENTION TO YOUR PRESS TOUR.
TED BARTON WILL ANNOUNCE YOU INTEND TO SET THE WORLD RECORD FOR THE MOST INTERVIEWS IN ONE HOUR. WE'LL CALL IT "MEDIA BLITZ!"
THERE'S A RECORD FOR THAT?
TED BARTON DOESN'T CARE! IT'S JUST A HOOK. YOU'LL GET MAXIMUM NATIONAL COVERAGE FOR MINIMUM EFFORT, THEN WE'LL DO THE WHOLE CIRCUIT ON FOLLOW-UP STORIES.
THE MESSAGE? "TEENAGE SUPER-HEROES ARE YOUR FRIENDS!"
MY PEOPLE WILL FAX PRESS KITS AND AN ITINERARY TO TV AND RADIO STATIONS ALL OVER THE COUNTRY.
TELL 'EM NOT TO BOTHER. I JUST RAN THAT STUFF OVER TO ALL THE STATIONS IN PERSON.
WHOOSH
YOU-- YOU JUST...
TED BARTON THINKS THIS PLAN IS DEFINITELY GOING TO WORK.

THERE'S NO LOGIC TO THIS SCHEDULE. OUR STOPS ZIGZAG BACK AND FORTH ACROSS THE COUNTRY.
YOU SHOULDN'T READ WHILE YOU'RE RUNNING, OR USE YOUR PORTABLE PLAYTENDO. TRUST ME.
I DON'T BELIEVE THIS. OUR FIRST INTERVIEW IS ON THE NEW BETHANY SNOW SHOW.
AND?
LET'S JUST SAY SHE'S NO FAN OF THE TITANS.
IMPULSE?
I'M RECEIVING. IS THAT YOU...
...RED TORNADO? HOW DO YOU LIKE BEING A KID?
IT'S THE FIRST TIME FOR ME. I THINK I'D ENJOY IT UNDER OTHER CIRCUM-STANCES.
HARD KORE! I GOT DA CRAZ FLOW
WE NEED YOU IN NORTH CAROLINA. A METAHUMAN CALLING HIMSELF MAJOR DISASTER DEMANDED A BILLION DOLLARS TO REFRAIN FROM SMASHING THE COAST WITH A TIDAL WAVE.
AS HE WAS ALREADY IN JAIL WHEN HE MADE THE THREAT, IT WAS DISMISSED AS A BLUFF.
THAT DOES NOT APPEAR TO HAVE BEEN AN ACCURATE ASSESSMENT.
KA-POW! BOOM! BOOM! ON EVERY FOE. HARD KORE! I GOT DA CRAZ FLOW!
WE'RE ON IT!

THAT IS ONE BIG TIDAL WAVE...

IT'S ONLY ABOUT A MINUTE AND A HALF FROM SHORE. HOW DO YOU WANT TO HANDLE IT?

UMMM...

WHAT WOULD GRANDPA DO? WHAT WOULD GRANDPA DO?

BUILD RETAINING WALL OF SANDBAGS.

DIG GIANT TRENCH TO STOP WAVE.

CREATE WIND VORTEX, REDIRECT WATER.

DIG HOLE IN OCEAN FLOOR, LET WATER DRAIN.

GATHER MILLIONS OF SPONGES, ABSORB WAVE.

EVACUATE ENTIRE COAST BY CARRYING EVERYONE OUT AT SUPER-SPEED.

TRAVEL BACK IN TIME, PREVENT TIDAL WAVE FROM EVER OCCURRING.

WHAT WAS WITH YOU BACK THERE?
I DON'T KNOW, THERE WERE SO MANY OPTIONS. I NEVER REALIZED BEFORE...
WELL, GET ON THE STICK, BART. WE GOT A LOT TO DO TODAY. GOTHAM CITY NEXT...
YOU SEE BATMAN? NO MATTER WHAT HAPPENS, SOMEHOW IT'S ALWAYS BUSINESS AS USUAL WITH HIM.
MAYBE IT'S BECAUSE HE STAYS FOCUSED ON THE PROBLEM AT HAND. YOU SHOULD TRY THAT SOMETIME, WALLY.
LOOK, YOUR VIDEO CLIPS WERE GREAT, MR. RYDER--
CALL ME JACK.
GREAT, SOMEBODY OUGHT TO TRY TO GIVE THOSE GUYS A FAIR SHAKE.
WELL, HERE'S THE DEAL, JACK. CONSIDER THIS A TEST. IF YOU REALLY DELIVER THE LIVE FLASH INTERVIEW YOU PROMISED ME, YOU'RE HIRED.
HOLD UP--LOOK AT THOSE GUYS OUTSIDE THE STATION. THEY'RE A.P.E.S.*
MAN, THERE'S PROBABLY A WARRANT OUT FOR YOU BY NOW.
*ALL PURPOSE ESPIONAGE SQUAD.
IT WAS SO HELPFUL OF US TO SUPPLY THEM WITH OUR ITINERARY, WALLY. BET THEY GOT SOME ANTI-SPEED STUFF, TOO.
WE DON'T WANT TO ENDANGER THE PEOPLE WORKING THERE, BART. WE BETTER SKIP THIS ONE. LET'S GET OVER TO METROPOLIS.
MBC
"YEAH. IT'S ONLY ONE LITTLE INTERVIEW. NO HARM DONE."
I WISH I HAD OFFICIALLY HIRED YOU, THEN I COULD OFFICIALLY FIRE YOU.

JUST FILL UP THE BAG, UNLESS YOU WANT A FACE FULL OF WHAT THOSE GUARDS GOT.
I CAN EMIT ANY KIND OF GAS THERE IS. SUCH IS THE POWER OF THE GREEN CIGARETTE!
BANK
FWOOSH
UH-OH. DID SOMEBODY JUST PUT OUT MY HEAD?
BANK
LET ME GET THIS STRAIGHT-- HE WAS HAVING TOO MUCH TROUBLE WITH SUPER-HEROES IN ALABAMA, SO HE MOVES TO METROPOLIS?
YOU'RE GOING TO HAVE TO SHOW ME HOW YOU DID THAT, SOMETIME.
COF, COF
HAK! KAF! KAFF!
"MAYBE AFTER THE PRESS CONFERENCE..."
LOIS LANE, DAILY PLANET. MY SOURCES SAY THAT YOUNG JUSTICE'S DESTRUCTION WASN'T MERELY A WILLFUL ACT OF VANDALISM. WOULD YOU CARE TO COMMENT?
WE APPRECIATE THE FORUM, MS. LANE. WE'RE NOT GUILTY OF ANYTHING, AND WE DON'T LIKE LOOKING GUILTY. WHAT REALLY HAPPENED--
ALL RIGHT YOU TWO, HOLD IT!
WE'VE GOT A WARRANT FOR YOUR ARREST! YOU'RE COMING WITH US!
THEY'RE ALREADY GONE, MAN.
I HAD A FOLLOW-UP.
I STOPPED OFF TO GET SOME GUYS OUT OF A BURNING BUILDING. WHO YOU CALLING?
I READ THE LOCAL PAPER WHILE I WAS WAITING FOR YOU AND IT GAVE ME AN IDEA...

"--THERE'S THIS NEWSPAPER REPORTER IN TOWN WHO WROTE SOME PRETTY FAIR STUFF ABOUT SUPERMAN. MAYBE HE CAN HELP US DO A LITTLE DAMAGE CONTROL..."
THIS IS CLARK KENT AT THE DAILY PLANET. I CAN'T COME TO THE PHONE RIGHT NOW. PLEASE LEAVE A MESSAGE.

MR. KENT? THIS IS IMPULSE. I'VE GOT SOME INSIDE INFORMATION ON THE JLA JUNIOR STORY. I'LL CALL YOU BACK LATER. LET'S TALK.
ANY LUCK?
NAH, YOU KNOW HOW LAZY REPORTERS ARE...

DAILY PLA
"...KENT'S PROBABLY HOLED-UP SOMEPLACE SLEEPING OFF A THREE-MARTINI LUNCH."*
*ACTUALLY, HE'S FIGHTING MATCH IN SUPERMAN, JR. / SUPERBOY, SR. #1!

WE'RE NOT DOING SO GOOD.
SURE WE ARE. WE STOPPED THE EARTHQUAKE AND THE TIDAL WAVE, CAUGHT ALL THOSE CROOKS, KEPT THE AIRPLANE FROM CRASHING, GOT THAT BOMB OFF THE HUB CITY ARCH...

I WAS TALKING ABOUT THE INTERVIEWS. BESIDES, I DID MOST OF THAT STUFF BY MYSELF WHILE YOU STOOD AROUND THINKING, OR OGLING GIRLS...
I KNOW, I'M SORRY, IT'S JUST, I FEEL LIKE I CAN'T MAKE ANY MISTAKES NOW.
"SORRY" DON'T CUT IT IN OUR BUSINESS.

HEY! I'M NOT THE ONE WHO YELLED AT KATIE COURIC! I'M NOT THE ONE WHO TOLD RUSH THAT THE HALF A BRAIN HE HAS TIED BEHIND HIS BACK DIED FROM LACK OF USE! I'M NOT THE ONE WHO DE-PANTSED ROY RAYMOND JR.!
AND I WAS NOT LOOKING AT GIRLS, EITHER.

SPEAKING OF GIRLS, LONG AS WE'RE HERE IN GATEWAY CITY, I'M GOING TO CHECK UP ON A COUPLE OF MY FAVORITES.

EVERYTHING UNDER CONTROL, DIANA?
AS WELL AS COULD BE EXPECTED. WE'RE OFF TO BATTLE A CYCLOPS.* IN TOWN FOR ANOTHER INTERVIEW?
*SEE WONDER GIRLS #1.
LAST ONE, JAQUELINE CABRERO, KGCW-TV. KNOW HER?
SO BART, WHAT DO YOU...
HEY... BART?
UM, UH, UH, UM...
NOT QUITE SO IMPULSIVE NOW, EH?
I GUESS, BUT I CAN'T BELIEVE YOU'RE LOUNGING AROUND HERE, CONSIDERING EVERYTHING THAT'S HAPPENING IN YOUR HOMETOWN.
WHAT ARE YOU TALKING ABOUT?
HUH?

"KEYSTONE CITY. THE FOLDED MAN'S BACK IN TOWN. IT'S BEEN ON TV ALL MORNING. DON'T YOU EVER WATCH THE NEWS?"
YOU KNOW SOME INTERESTING PEOPLE, WALLY.
MAYBE I SHOULD THROW A BARBECUE. LISTEN UP, THIS IS NORMAN BRIDGE'S HOUSE.

THE SOFTWARE BILLIONAIRE?
YEAH. HE'S BEEN HUNTING DOWN A FORMER EMPLOYEE WHO CALLS HIMSELF "THE FOLDED MAN" BECAUSE HE CAN TRAVEL THROUGH HIGHER DIMENSIONS.
LOOKS LIKE HE FOUND HIM. WHAT'S THE PLAN?

TELL YOU WHAT, GENERAL PATTON--YOU STAY HERE AND THINK OF ONE. I'M GOING IN THERE, GRAB BRIDGES AND GET HIM OUT.

PLEASE, GAUSS. WHAT DO YOU WANT FROM ME?
YOU TELL ME. YOU'RE THE ONE WHO PUT A PRICE ON MY HEAD. WELL, I'M HERE, SO PAY UP!
MONEY? YOU JUST WANT MONEY? I'LL PAY.

OH, YOU'LL PAY, ALL RIGHT.
I'M GOING TO DROP YOU AND YOUR HOUSE SOMEWHERE ROUGHLY EQUIDISTANT BETWEEN SUBSPACE AND FLATLAND.
ALL RIGHT, GAUSS. THAT'S ENOUGH.
KID FLASH? DON'T I RATE THE REAL THING?

I'M MORE THAN ENOUGH FLASH TO HANDLE YOUUHHNN!
THEN BY ALL MEANS, BIG BOY, COME GET ME.

WHAT THE HEEEEE...?
OH, HEY WALLY, COME HERE A MINUTE, WILL YOU?

NOT RIGHT NOW. I'VE GOT A FOLDED MAN TO SPINDLE AND --

--MUTILATE?
WHAT THE...? I WAS JUST INSIDE, RUNNING RIGHT AT HIM!
THAT'S NOT GONNA WORK.

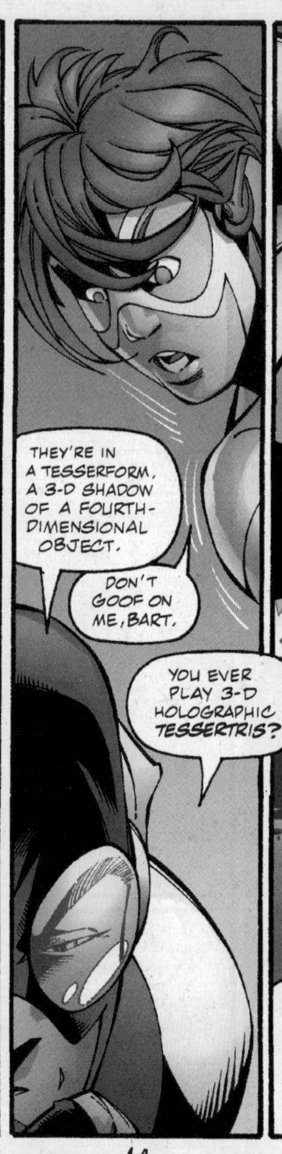
THEY'RE IN A TESSERFORM, A 3-D SHADOW OF A FOURTH-DIMENSIONAL OBJECT.
DON'T GOOF ON ME, BART.
YOU EVER PLAY 3-D HOLOGRAPHIC TESSERTRIS?

NO.
WELL, I HAVE. IN THE 30TH CENTURY IT'S A VERY POPULAR GAME. AND I'M REALLY GOOD AT IT.

IF THIS IS ANYTHING LIKE THE GAME, THAT WHOLE HOUSE AND HALF THIS COUNTY ARE ABOUT TO GO DOWN THE DRAIN.
PLAN?
I'M SO GLAD YOU ASKED. FOLLOW MY LEAD. IF THIS WORKS, WE'RE NOT GOING TO HAVE MUCH TIME TO GET EVERYBODY OUT.

...AND THIS WAS THE SCENE AT NORMAN BRIDGES' ESTATE. FLASH AND KID FLASH, ZOOMING IN AND OUT OF THE STRUCTURE, OFTEN MOVING FASTER THAN THE EYE COULD FOLLOW, APPARENTLY RANDOMLY REARRANGING FURNITURE.
THE TWO FLASHES EVACUATED NEARLY THREE DOZEN OF MR. BRIDGES' EMPLOYEES, AND MR. BRIDGES HIMSELF, ONLY MOMENTS BEFORE THE ESTATE VANISHED FOREVER INTO WHAT S.T.A.R. LABS OFFICIALS DESCRIBED AS A "WORMHOLE."

MOST EVACUEES HAD NOTHING BUT PRAISE FOR THE HEROES. NORMAN BRIDGES HAD A DIFFERENT TAKE ON THE DAY'S EVENTS...
ALL I KNOW IS THAT THE FLASH DESTROYED MY HOUSE AND THAT MY KIDNAPPER GOT AWAY.
WE'LL GET HIM NEXT TIME.
BART, THAT STUFF YOU DID IN THE HOUSE WAS AMAZING. YOU'RE SAYING WE PLUGGED UP THE WORMHOLE JUST BY MOVING THE FURNITURE AROUND?
KLIK
AND A COUPLE OF WALLS. IT'S NO BIG DEAL. IT WAS JUST LIKE LEVEL 18 OF SUPER-TESSERTRIS.
IT'S A SHAME NOBODY REALLY UNDERSTANDS WHAT HAPPENED.
HALF THE STATIONS ARE SAYING WE DEMOLISHED THE PLACE FOR NO REASON. FRANKLY, THAT'S HOW IT LOOKED TO ME.
MAN, THIS WHOLE EXERCISE WAS A BUST.
WHATEVER WE TRIED TO DO TODAY, WE ENDED UP HELPING A LOT OF PEOPLE. THAT'S OUR REAL WORK, AND IT'S WAY MORE IMPORTANT THAN HOW WE LOOK.
"WE'VE GOT A RESPONSIBILITY TO SERVE THE PUBLIC, WHETHER THEY THINK WE'RE SWELL GUYS OR NOT."
SECURITY
WHAT?
NOTHING, IT'S JUST RIGHT NOW?
YEAH?
YOU REMIND ME OF BARRY.

LATER...

CAPTAIN COLD! A MOMENT OF YOUR TIME?

WHERE'D YOU COME FROM? WHO ARE YOU?

From the journal of Courtney Whitmore...
I though it'd be YEARS until I saw the STARS.
And in a really screwed-up way, it HAS been.
I used to be nicknamed the Star-Spangled Kid, 16 year-old "cheerleader" of the Justice Society of America.
But the "KID" part fell off after I was zapped by this witchboy, Klarion, AND, at the same time, shot by Doiby Dickles' "de-aging" gun--
--along with the REST of the JSA.
The mixture of science and magic changed me into a STARWOMAN, and left the others younger than I used to be.
NOW I'm at least 25. Maybe 26.
That's SO old.
...I'm flying into space, aboard the USA's STEEL EAGLE--
--off to ANOTHER PLANET to find the CURE. Another one of Doiby's "de-aging" guns.
But until that "cure" is found, I'm in charge--
But I can't worry about MYSELF right now. There's MORE important things at stake. My teammates. My stepfather. The world, too.
And since this mixture of magic and science is keeping Hourman's time vision and Fate's sorcery from switching us back to our proper ages...
KSSSH
HEY, THAT'S MY BLACKOUT BOMB!

STAR-
WOMAN
JSA's ROLL CALL

TEEN
LANTERN

GOLDEN AGE
KID FLASH

WILDBRAT

SANDY THE
GOLDEN BOY

CRYBABY
LI'L FATE
--And the members of the JSA are MY RESPONSIBILITY!
STARS and TYKES
I'm a superhero babysitter in charge of a metahuman preschool class. One on a constant sugar rush.
I WANNA GO HOME!
TOTALLY OFF, MAN! POWER GIRL'S WAY HOTTER!
FACE THE WRATH OF A CHAMPION, PUNK!
ARRH!
WE CAN FIGURE OUT HOW THIS WORKS, TERRIFIC! I JUST NEED TO TAKE IT APART!
GEOFF JOHNS
WORD BOY
DREW JOHNSON
PENCIL LAD
RICH FABER &
RODNEY RAMOS
INKIN' BOYS
JOE ROSAS
COLOR KID

BIGG BOY

HAWKBABY

HOURBOY

KID MID-NITE

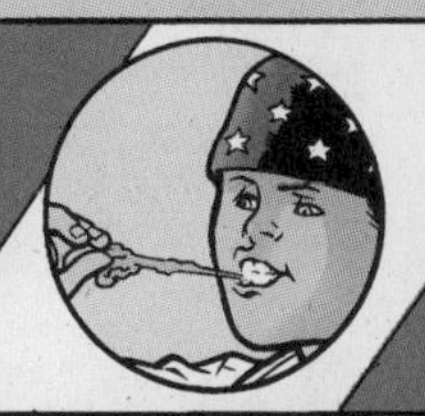

STAR-SPANGLED KID

TERRIFIC LAD

S.T.R.I.P.E.S.Y., MERRY-GIRL OF 1,000 GIMMICKS, and DOIBY DICKLES

SHE'S THE ONE THAT SWIPED MID-NITE'S SMOKE BOMB!
YEAH. THAT WAS MINE.
KENDRA, DON'T TAKE THINGS THAT AREN'T YOURS. ESPECIALLY WEAPONS. OKAY?
NARC.
CHECK THIS OUT, TEDDY!
SAY IT AGAIN, HOURBOY! C'MON!
I AM A MACHINE COLONY FROM THE 853RD CENTURY, PROGRAMMED WITH MIRACLO-ENHANCED D.N.A. OF THE ORIGINAL--
YOU'RE A DOUGHBOY IS WHAT YOU ARE!
I'M NOT A DOUGH-BOY.
LEAVE THE ANDROID ALONE, GUYS.
GET LOST, OLD LADY. WHO NEEDS YA?
LISTEN, JACK, YOU LITTLE--
STOP THAT, PLEASE!
PAT! MIKE! DON'T TAKE HOURBOY APART!
WHAT? I WAS JUST LOOKIN'. SEE WHAT MAKES THIS "MACHINE COLONY" WORK.
YEAH. WHAT MAKES THIS JOKER TICK AND TOCK?
'SIDES. YOU'RE JUST MY STEPDAUGHTER. YOU CAN'T TELL ME WHAT TO DO.
BEEP! BEEP BEEP BEEP!
OH, BROTHER. I KNEW I SHOULDA LEFT YOU BEHIND.
IN CASE YOU FORGOT, I'M THE ONE THAT BUILT THIS SHIP. WITHOUT ME YOU ARE SCREWED IF ANYTHING BREAKS DOWN! HAHA!
GIMME MY HELMET BACK!
KENDRA!
FINDERS KEEPERS, LOSERS WEEPERS!

GEE, I REMEMBER MYRG, DOIBY. IT SURE WAS SWELL FOR AN ALIEN PLANET.
THANKS TO YOU, THE BROOKLYN I REMEMBER WHEN WE WERE PALLING AROUND BACK IN THE 30'S STILL EXISTS.
SAD TA SAY THINGS'VE CHANGED SINCE I WAS BACK THERE, LANTRIN. MY PRINCESS--
IS IT MUCH LONGER, DOIBY? I DON'T KNOW IF I CAN TAKE THIS CONSTANT CHATTERING ANYMORE.
EVEN WITH MY IMPAIRED HEARING.
I'M WITH HER. LET'S GET THAT AGING GUN AND PROPEL THESE TYKES PAST PUBERTY...
...AND MERRY... I KNOW THIS ISN'T THE TIME, BUT I'D REALLY LIKE TO HEAR ABOUT SYLVESTER PEMBERTON.
THE FIRST STAR-SPANGLED KID -- YOUR BROTHER.
THERE'S SO MUCH I DON'T KNOW AND SO MUCH I WANT--
LOOK, "STARWOMAN." OR WHATEVER YOU'RE GOING TO CALL YOURSELF NOW...
MY BROTHER DIED A TRUE HERO, AND AS FAR AS I'M CONCERNED, YOU'RE DESTROYING HIS MEMORY. PAT DIDN'T CHOOSE YOU TO BECOME A NEW "STAR-SPANGLED KID." YOU STOLE THE BELT.
YOU KIDS TODAY DON'T KNOW STEP ONE ABOUT BEING A HERO. YOU HAVE NO SENSE OF LEGACY OR HONOR. NO RESPECT FOR WHAT'S GONE ON BEFORE.
BUT I...
THE ONLY REASON I'M HERE IS TO HELP DOIBY AND THE OTHERS. NOT YOU.
GRAV ON
HEY, GANG, WATCH THIS -- EVERY-ONE'S GONNA BE ABLE TO FLY NOW!!
HAWKBABY! NO!
YOUSURE YOUWANNADO THAT? SOMEONE MIGHTGET--
COOL!

FWHHHJJJJJMMMMMMMM
MY GLASSES! I CAN'T SEE!
LOOK AT ME! I CAN FLY!
LEMME DOWN! LEMME DOWN!
WHY DO YOU KEEP SPOILING ALL OUR FUN?
KNOCK IT OFF, GUYS.
THIS ISN'T A GAME. IT'S SERIOUS STUFF.
FWUMP
WHOOOOOSH
DO YOU WANT TO STAY LIKE THIS?
SURE! WHY NOT? GETTING OLDER SUCKS.
WATCH YOUR LANGUAGE.
TOLD HER NOT TO DO IT!
WHABOOM
SOMETHING JUST HIT THE STEEL EAGLE!
WHAT THE HELL WAS IT?
WATCH MY LANGUAGE?

WHAM
HANG ON, YOUSE GUYS! ASTEROIDS INCOMIN'!
GEE! I DON'T REMEMBER THIS PLANET HAVING A RING OF ASTEROIDS ORBITING IT.
IT DIDN'T USETA. I TOLDJA. THINGS CHANGED.
I USETA BE KING O' THAT HUNK O' DOIT.
KING? YOU?
UNTIL DE PLANET GREN INVADED IT. THEIR FOIST ATTACK BUSTED UP THE MOON 'ERE. LEFT THAT ASTEROID WAVE IN ITS PLACE.
THE ONLY WAY TO KEEP ANYONE FROM GETTIN' HOIT WAS TO CONSUMMATE A PEACE TREATY BY MARRIAGE. AND MY LOVELY PRINCESS RAMIA WAS FORCED TA WED PRINCE MARIEB OF GREN --
-- AND FORGET ALL ABOUT DOIBY DICKLES.
SHE SURE WAS PRETTY, DOIBY. BUT DON'T WORRY! WE'LL FIX EVERYTHING!
ANYONE SEE MY GLASSES?
SAFETY FIRST, TROOPS! BETTER BUCKLE UP FAST AND PREPARE FOR LANDING!
OUT OF MY WAY, SMALL FRY.
YA BIG BULLY! I CAN'T SEE!
Terra

"PLANET MYRG, HERE WE COME!"
WATCH WHERE YER DRIVIN', YA MOOKS!
TAXI
CLARKAB
WHEEP WHEEP
FABER PORTER

BOY, I REALLY MISS CENTRAL PARK. BE-YOO-TIFUL!
AND IT'LL MAKE A GOOD COVER FOR THE SHIP.
OKAY, JSA. LET'S ALL STICK TOGETHER.
MAYBE WE SHOULD HOLD HANDS. BUDDY SYSTEM. SAFETY IN NUMBERS.
EEEWWW. LET GO, BIGG BOY!
DAT'S THE JOINT WHERE THE GUN IS – THE ROYAL PALACE. THERE'S ONE IN THE ARMORY. T'IRD FLOOR.
ROYAL PALACE
PALACE
WELL, WHATARE WEWAITINGFOR? LET'SGOGOGO GOGOGO!
PLACE IS LOADED WITH COPS, SPEEDY. WE'RE GONNA HAVE TO SNEAK IN THE BACK DOOR. SO FOLLOW ME.
CRUNCH CRUNCH CRUNCH
NEAT.
CHECK THIS OUT, DUDE!
FREE COTTON CANDY!
AWESOME!
BEEP! BEEP BEEP!
NEW CONEY ISLAND
LET'S DITCH THESE LOSERS!
HEY! YOU GUYS GET BACK HERE! THAT'S AN ORDER FROM THE CHAIRMAN OF THE JSA!!
BITE ME, MR. CHAIRMAN!
NEW CONEY ISLAND
HEY, WAIT FOR ME! I'M COMIN' TOO!
HOLO VIDEO
I USETA BE KING. NOW I'M A WANTED MAN. IT JUST AIN'T FAIR.
WANTED
I THINK WE'RE MISSING SOME CHILDREN.
OH, MAN. WHERE'S PAT? MOM'S GONNA KILL ME!

SYLVESTER NEVER LOST ANYONE. HE KNEW WHAT BEING RESPONSIBLE WAS ALL--
I'M NOT SYLVESTER, OKAY! I'M NOT TRYING TO BE SYLVESTER!
QUIET, YOUSE GUYS! SAVE IT FER LATER! WE DON'T WANNA--
FREEZE!
DOIBY DICKLES! YOUS'RE UNDER ARREST FOR TREASON AGAINST PRINCE MARIEB AN' THE PLANET MYRG!
AN' SO ARE YER FRIENDS! GIVE 'EM THE STUN TREAT-MENT, BOYS!
--ATTRACT ANY ATTENTION... D'OH.
KZZZZT
BOY, THEY'RE GONNA GET IT WHEN I TELL STARWOMAN THEY DITCHED--
OPEN
PRINCE MARIEB'S GONNA GIVE US A NICE FAT BONUS! GOOD WORK!
RATZIS!
THEY'VE BEEN CAPTURED!
WHAT IN THE WIDE WORLD OF MYRG AM I GONNA DO NOW?

BY ORDER OF THE CAPITAL BLUE BOYS, I'M PROUD TO PRESENT THE CAPTURE OF MYRG'S #1 ENEMY-- DOIBY DICKLES!!
AND NOW... ALL HAIL PRINCE MARIEB AND PRINCESS RAMIA!!
HAIL!
YAY!
DEATH TO DOIBY DICKLES!
DAMN. THEY TOOK MY COSMIC ROD.
THIS IS ALL YOUR FAULT.
WHAT?!
DOIBY DICKLES. I WISH I COULD SAY THIS IS AN UNEXPECTED SURPRISE. BUT IT'S NOT.
I KNEW YA COULDN'T STAY AWAY FOR LONG. YOUR TINY MENTAL CAVITY WON'T ALLOW YA TA PROCESS HOW VITAL THIS MARRIAGE IS TA MYRG'S SURVIVAL.
AND THE PENALTY FOR CONTINUALLY TRYING TA "ANNUL" THIS ARRANGEMENT IS DEATH.
THE SENTENCE TA BE CARRIED OUT IMMEDIATELY.
HIZ ROYALNESS
OH, DOIBY, MY LOVE. I TOLD YA NOT TA COME BACK.
PRINCESS! I LOVES YA! I DO! AND WE'RE GONNA FIND SOME WAY TA GET THESE INVADING SCUM OFFA OUR PLANET.
YOU'RE GONNA KILL ALL OF US, HUH? I DOUBLE DARE YA!
I SEE OUR HEALTH IS IMPORTANT TO YOU, LANTERN!
INDEED!
HRM.
DARE AXCEPTED, YOUNG MAN.
HERMAN. IF YA WOULD...

KLANK
UH, OH...
BETTER TAKE A SEAT, NARC!
AAAAAAHHHH!!!
ILIKEIT ILIKEIT!! WHEEEE!!
BOOOYAA!

CRIPES! HATE TO SAY THE LITTLE GUY'S RIGHT, BUT WE BETTER GO HELP THEM!
LET ME *BORROW* THAT COSMIC CONVERTER BELT, KID!
JUST FOR A MINUTE, THOUGH!

ALL RIGHT, S.T.R.I.P.E.-- LET'S GET A HYDRO-STARLIGHT ENGINE ON THIS COASTER *FAST!*
AND DON'T FORGET THE *PROPULSION BRAKES!*
BEEP! *BEEP BEEP BEEP!*
WHAT'D HE SAY?

HE SAID, "*OF COURSE* I WON'T FORGET THE PROPULSION BRAKES."
ZWIP
ZWIP
ZWIP
ZWIP

YEAH!!
KLANK
COOL!! A FLYING ROLLER COASTER!
LET'S GO HAND OUT SOME BEATINGS! JSA STYLE!
NEW CONEY ISLAND
VRARAMRAMRAMRAM

I SHOULDN'T HAVE DRAGGED YOUSE INTA THIS MESS, LANTRIN!
HEY, THAT'S OKAY, DOIBY. WE'VE BEEN PALS FOR OVER SIXTY YEARS. AND PALS ALWAYS STICK TOGETHER.
HEY, HOURBOY, WHAT ARE THEY DOING? I CAN'T SEE A THING!
I BELIEVE THEY INTEND ON DELVING INTO OUR ENTRAILS WITH AN AXE.
FATE. LISTEN TO ME FOR A SECOND.
Y-YEAH?
I KNOW YOU DON'T THINK YOU CAN USE YOUR POWERS. BUT YOU REALLY REALLY REALLY GOTTA TRY.
THE JSA NEEDS YOU, FATE. YOUR FRIENDS NEED YOU.
AND I KNOW YOU CAN DO IT. I BELIEVE IN YOU.
Y-YOU DO?
COURTNEY'S RIGHT, FATE! YOU JUST NEED SOME SELF-CONFIDENCE!
I DON'T--
YOU'RE DR. FATE! ONE OF THE MOST POWERFUL SORCERERS IN THE UNIVERSE!!
Y-YEAH!! A SPELL FROM THE WITCH'S RED FLOWER GARDEN WILL TAKE CARE OF THESE STUPID CHAINS!
THANKS, NABU!
SHRINGG
ALL RIGHT!! WAY TO GO, FATE!
RARRR!
HEY, TALL, DARK AND GRUESOME!
NO! GET THEM!
KILL THEM!
ANNIHILATE THEM!!

BEEP! BEEP BEEP BEEP!
WAZZZUP?!
WHEEEEEE!!!
KA-BAMMM

YOUSE KEEP THESE JOKERS BUSY WHILE LANTRIN AND I GRAB THAT GUN! IT WON'T TAKE BUT A MINUTE!
YOU WON'T GET VERY FAR, LITTLE MAN!
DOIBY, LOOK OUT!
COURTNEY! THE ROD RESPONDS TO MENTAL COMMANDS! YOU GOTTA WILL IT TO YOU BEFORE HE ZAPS HIM!
FWASSHT
AAH!
WHAT A RUSH. MAKES YOU A LITTLE DIZZY.
THANKS, JACK.
NOW LET'S GIVE THEM A LESSON IN COSMIC ENERGY YOUR DAD WOULD BE PROUD OF!
BWASTT
THAT'S RIGHT! DON'T MESS WITH THE BEST! BOOOYAA!
PICK YOUR FIGHTS CAREFULLY! WE JUST NEED TO KEEP THEM BUSY UNTIL THEY GET THE GUN! AND REMEMBER, WE'RE THE JSA, SO--
--STICK TOGETHER!

SOMEONECOULD GETHURT WRESTLINGWITH YOU!
WHAP
WHAP
WHAP
WHAP
WHY DON'T YOU TAKE ON SOMEONE YOUR OWN SIZE, GIGANTO!!
WHOA!
RHT!
VWOOSHH
YO! HE'S NOT PLAYING FAIR WITH THAT AXE!
TAKE IT OUT, S.T.R.I.P.E.!
BEEP! BEEPBEEP BEEP!
VWIP
VWIP
VWIP
VWIP
VWIP
LET'S PIN THIS BUFFOON!
HURM?
CLANG
KINK

GO GET HIM!
YOU'RE THE ONLY ONE WHO CAN SEE IN DARK!
BUT I'M S-SCARED OF THE DARK!
FORGET HIM! THAT HUGE EXECUTIONER GUY IS TAKING OUR FRIENDS OUT LIKE PAPER DOLLS!
LET'S CREAM HIM!
KRAK
THAT THE BEST YOU GOT, WIMP?
OOOF!
ARGHH!!!
WE GOT THE GUN!
BUT WE GOT MORE COMPANY TOO!!
BRING 'EM ON!
YEAH!!
WE CAN TAKE ON ANY--

THOSE'RE THE MOOKS WHO BEAT UP HERMAN!
GET 'EM!!
BA-BOOOM
I'LL BE BACK, PRINCESS! I PROMISE!

I LOVES YA, DOIBY DICKLES!

THE JUNIOR JSA IS OUTTA HERE!
PAARR
I CAN'T WAIT TO USE THIS THING, DOIBY.
PAT AND MIKE, YOU'RE GOOD AT FIGURING TECH STUFF OUT, SO--
Aww.
PHYSICS
PALMER
NAP TIME, huh?
I SUPPOSE WE CAN =YAWN= SORT THIS OUT... IN A FEW MINUTES...

I fell FAST like a STAR. That's the last thing I remember until I woke up on Earth.
It'd been a FANTASTIC adventure. I hate to use the word "eye-opener"-- because it was so much MORE than that.
For everyone, I think.
And I've never been prouder to be a member of the USA-- regardless of what my "code name" is...
...or WILL be.
WHAT?
YOU'RE A SOFTY, AIN'T YA, GIMMICK GIRL.
OH, FIDDLE-FADDLE!
SHE MIGHT BE COLD. NOW PUT THE PEDAL TO THE METAL AND GET US BACK HOME.
WE'VE GOT PRESSING MATTERS TO ATTEND TO!
VRROOOARRRRR

EARTH. UPSTATE NEW YORK.
A LEVEL 8 D.E.O. HOSPITAL CONTAINS A VERY SPECIAL PRISONER.
THE DOCTORS ARE STILL TRYING TO FIND A WAY TO REMOVE THAT TUMOR, DIRECTOR BONES, BUT--
UNTIL THEN YOU LEAVE THAT SONIC INHIBITOR AROUND HIS THROAT. IT TOOK THE ENTIRE JSA TO BRING BLACK ADAM IN LAST TIME, AGENT CHASE.*
*JSA #6.
KLARION!? THE WITCH BOY?
WHAMPF
AH! CAMERON CHASE. I KNEW WE'D MEET AGAIN. HOW'S KNOB?
FINE.
CRRMMBDLL
I'M JUST HERE TO BORROW THIS FRIEND OF YOURS.
AWAKEN, MY GOOD MAN... AND SPEAK MY NAME. KLARION.
K-KLARION?
SPLENDID! SIMPLY SPLENDID!
BLACK ADAM JR. WILL FIT RIGHT IN WITH THE OTHERS. AND AS FOR YOUR "OLD BONES"--
ZAPPY
ZAPPY
--LET'S FRESHEN THEM UP!
NOT A WORD OF THIS TO ANYONE.
GOTCHA, BOSS.

METROPOLIS. THE CITY OF TOMORROW...
...EARLIER TODAY...
OKAY, CYBER-SPIDER--OR WHATEVER YOU'RE CALLED--
I REALLY DON'T CARE WHAT I'M CALLED. I'M NOT INTERESTED IN NAMES.
WELL, YOU...YOU WERE SHOOTING UP THIS PLACE, CALLING OUT SUPERMAN, RIGHT?
SO CONSIDER YOUR CALL ANSWERED!
OKAY--BIT OF ADVICE? IF YOU USE A NAME--GET IT RIGHT.
YOU DON'T LOOK LIKE MUCH OF A SUPERMAN...
BWUM BWUM BWUM BWUM
...AND YOU SURE AREN'T FASTER THAN A SPEEDING BULLET!
GHHK--!
BWUM BWUM BWUM BWUM BWUM
I'D SAY WE GOT HERE JUST IN THE NICK O', MR. MORRIS!
WANT I SHOULD GET SOME SHOTS OF THE MAN OF STEEL FOR TONIGHT'S NEWSCAST?
HEY--LOOK! UP THERE, IN THE SKY--!
MAN OF STEEL? ISN'T THAT SUPERBOY OUT THERE, ANGIE? WHERE'S THE REAL SUPERMAN?

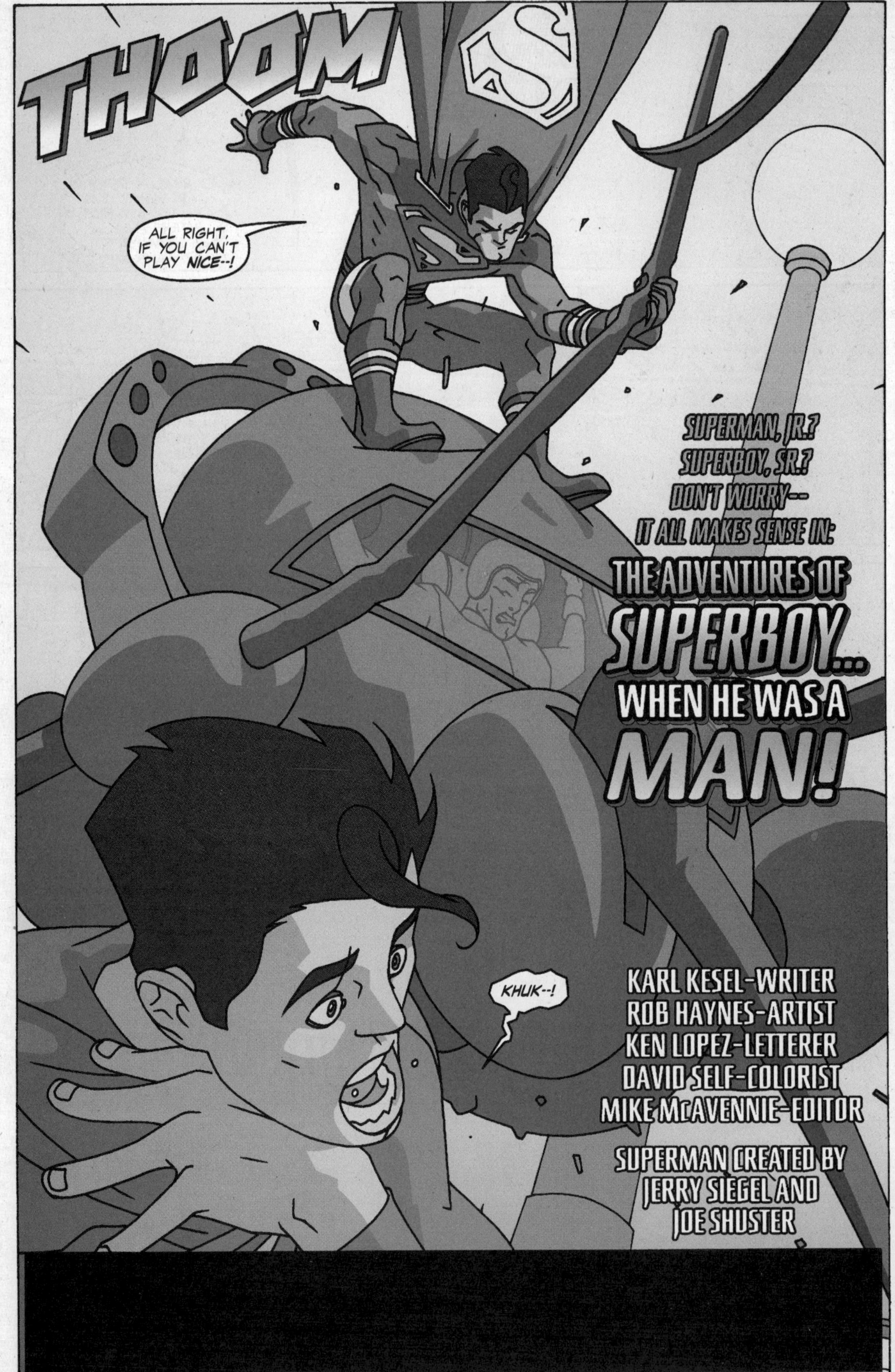
THOOM
ALL RIGHT, IF YOU CAN'T PLAY NICE--!
SUPERMAN, JR.?
SUPERBOY, SR.?
DON'T WORRY--
IT ALL MAKES SENSE IN:
THE ADVENTURES OF
SUPERBOY...
WHEN HE WAS A
MAN!
KHUK--!
KARL KESEL-WRITER
ROB HAYNES-ARTIST
KEN LOPEZ-LETTERER
DAVID SELF-COLORIST
MIKE McAVENNIE-EDITOR
SUPERMAN CREATED BY
JERRY SIEGEL AND
JOE SHUSTER

KREK

YOW! SKYWAY'S NOT BUILT FOR THROWDOWNS LIKE THIS!
AM I MISSING SOMETHING? WHY'S SUPERMAN DRESSED LIKE SUPERBOY, AND VICE VERSA?
MAYBE 'CAUSE OF THAT "JUSTICE FOR ALL" RALLY IN WASHINGTON, D.C.? Y'KNOW--TO SHOW KID HEROES AREN'T AS BAD AS YOU TV GUYS SAY.*
MAN--WISH MY GIRLFRIEND WAS HERE TO SEE THIS!
* FOR THE FULL STORY, SEE YOUNG JUSTICE: SINS OF YOUTH #1--STILL ON SALE, YOU LUCKY DEVIL!

SORRY, SUPERMAN...BOY... WHATEVER...
...THIS ISN'T OVER YET.
DIDN'T THINK IT WOULD BE.
SUPERMAN-- HOW YOU DOIN'?

KAAA--!
UM... NEVER BETTER!
BUT THAT'S THE LAST TIME I CATCH A BULLET IN MY TEETH.
LOOKS LIKE THE AGE-CHANGE CAUGHT UP WITH YOU, TOO, HUH? THAT WHY YOU'RE IN THE BIG APRICOT, SUPERBOY?

tZZZOK
THAT'S ONE REASONNGH!

SORRY. GOT DISTRACTED.
I'M OKAY.
CHOOM
ONE REASON? WHAT--JUST 'CAUSE I'M A LITTLE YOUNGER NOW, YOU THINK I CAN'T HANDLE THINGS ON MY OWN?
NOT FOR LONG.

LOOK--I DEAL WITH GUYS LIKE THIS ALL THE TIME! NO PROB---

buh-BWOOM

HOLY HINDENBURG!
JUST DESTROYED THE SKYWAY!
LUCKY NO ONE WAS HURT!
KID'S AS BAD AS THEY SAY!
DID YOU GET THAT, ANGIE? TELL ME YOU GOT THAT!

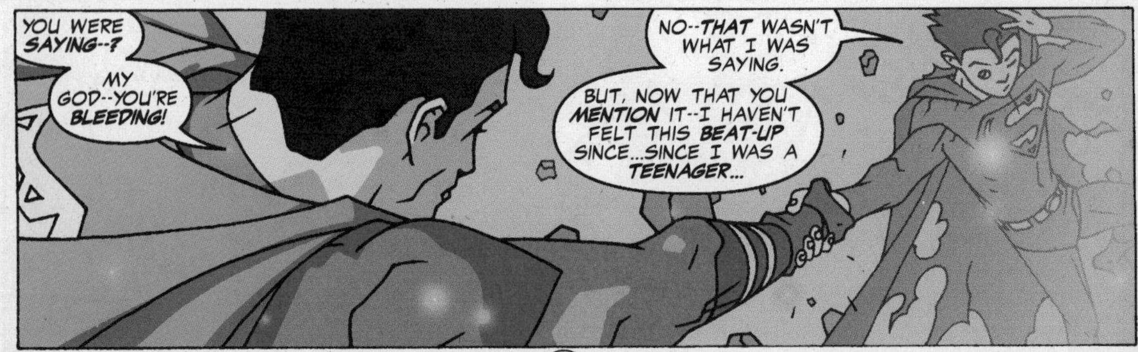
YOU WERE SAYING--?
MY GOD--YOU'RE BLEEDING!
NO--THAT WASN'T WHAT I WAS SAYING.
BUT, NOW THAT YOU MENTION IT--I HAVEN'T FELT THIS BEAT-UP SINCE...SINCE I WAS A TEENAGER...

...WHICH IS WHAT I AM! YEAH, OKAY--I GOT IT...
AND OUR ARMORED FRIEND'S ABOUT TO GET HIS!

FRSSH-KOOM

NNGH... RIGHT...LIKE I'M GOING ANYWHERE...
STAY WHERE YOU ARE! THIS IS THE POLICE! YOU'RE UNDER ARREST!
JUST IN TIME! ANY LONGER, THOSE TWO "HEROES" COULD'VE KILLED SOMEONE!
AND YOU SAW IT LIVE ON GBS! THIS IS MORRIE MORRIS, REPORTING FROM--

YOU CALL THAT REPORTING, MORRIS? EVER HEAR OF FACT-CHECKING? OR GETTING BOTH SIDES OF THE STORY?
MAYBE I SHOULD TEACH YOU A FEW THINGS ABOUT JOURNALISM!
I THINK YOU'VE HELPED HIM QUITE ENOUGH ALREADY, SUPERMAN.
I SUGGEST WE GET OUT OF HERE--WHILE WE STILL CAN.

THERE YOU HAVE IT, METROPOLIS--SUPERMAN AND SUPERBOY. IRRESPONSIBLE. RECKLESS.
PLAYING SOME TWISTED GAME OF THEIR OWN, WITH ABSOLUTELY NO CONCERN FOR WHO GETS HURT!

CONGRATULATIONS. I IMAGINE YOUR PARTING COMMENTS WILL LEAD TONIGHT'S NEWSCAST...
GIVE ME A BREAK! YOU DIDN'T EXACTLY HELP WITH THAT SUBTLE USE OF HEAT VISION BACK THERE!
AND SINCE WHEN DOES SUPERBOY HAVE HEAT VISION, ANYWAY?
WELL, I DIDN'T HAVE IT WHEN I WAS SIXTEEN--BUT NEITHER DID YOU, RIGHT? AND I'M SUPPOSED TO BE AS MUCH LIKE YOU AS POSSIBLE, SO NOW THAT I'M AN ADULT...
...I MIGHT HAVE OTHER POWERS I'M NOT USED TO, TOO--AND NOT BE ABLE TO CONTROL THEM ANY BETTER THAN THE HEAT VISION.
WAS HOPING YOU COULD HELP... 
OH-- YOU THINK YOU HAVE PROBLEMS?
AT LEAST YOU GOT WHAT YOU ALWAYS WANTED--TO BE SUPERMAN!
ME? I NEVER WAS SUPERBOY-- AND NEVER WANTED TO BE!

TELL ME! AND IT DOESN'T HELP THAT WHEN I WAS THIS AGE, MY ABILITIES JUST KEPT INCREASING! EVERY DAY I WAS A LITTLE BETTER AT...SOMETHING!
BUMBLING AROUND WITH CYBER-SPIDER BACK THERE--I FEEL LIKE I JUST FLUNKED THE MIDTERM!
WELL...A POP QUIZ, MAYBE.
IF IT MATTERS, I NEVER REALIZED HOW TOUGH ALL THESE NEW POWERS MUST HAVE BEEN FOR YOU TO ADJUST TO.
BET YOUR HEAT VISION ALMOST TORCHED YOUR HOME A DOZEN TIMES! GOOD THING YOU HAD PATIENT PARENTS!

...
YOU KNOW MY PARENTS?
UM... SURE.
JOR-EL AND LARA. ON KRYPTON.
NO. I MEAN...

LOOK, I'M GOING TO TELL YOU SOMETHING, OKAY? SOMETHING I SHOULD'VE TOLD YOU LONG AGO...
BUT IT'S A SECRET! A SUPER-SECRET YOU CAN'T TELL ANYONE!
SEE--I HAVE A SECRET IDENTITY. WHEN I'M NOT SUPERMAN, I AM...IN REALITY...
...CLARK KENT!
I KNOW.

YOU--?!
WELL, I KNEW YOU KNEW! I MEAN, I THOUGHT YOU KNEW! THAT'S THE ONLY REASON I TOLD YOU!
OR YOU WOULDN'T HAVE TOLD ME? EVER?
YES!
NO!
WHAT I MEAN IS--

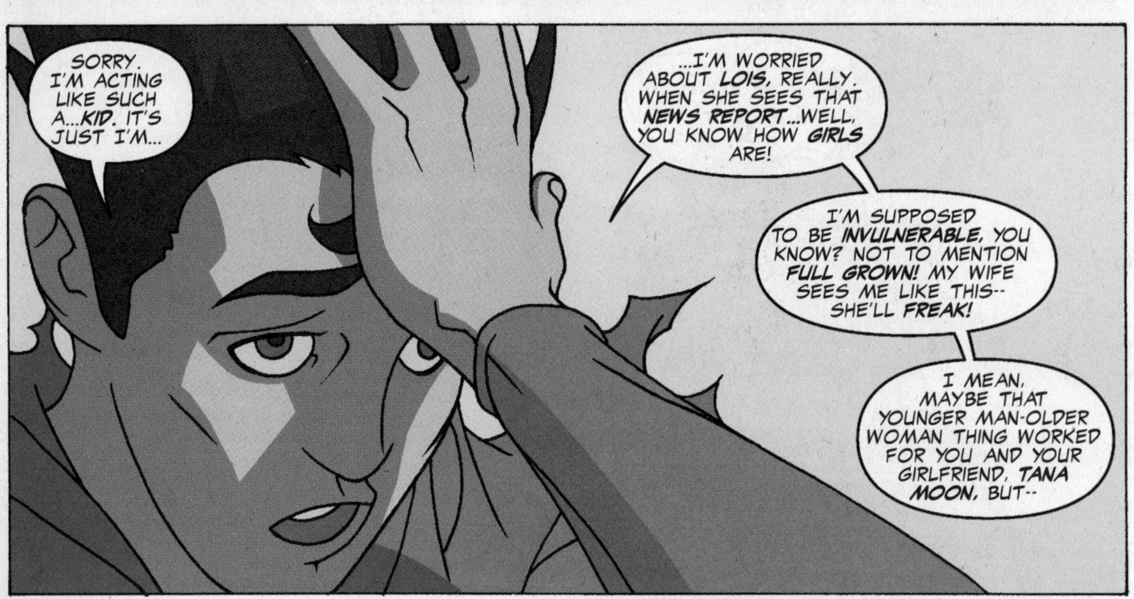
SORRY. I'M ACTING LIKE SUCH A...KID. IT'S JUST I'M...
...I'M WORRIED ABOUT LOIS, REALLY. WHEN SHE SEES THAT NEWS REPORT...WELL, YOU KNOW HOW GIRLS ARE!
I'M SUPPOSED TO BE INVULNERABLE, YOU KNOW? NOT TO MENTION FULL GROWN! MY WIFE SEES ME LIKE THIS-- SHE'LL FREAK!
I MEAN, MAYBE THAT YOUNGER MAN-OLDER WOMAN THING WORKED FOR YOU AND YOUR GIRLFRIEND, TANA MOON, BUT--

TANA'S DEAD.
SHE WAS KILLED A FEW HOURS AGO...

"...BY THE AGENDA."
...OUR ARMORED AGENT SUCCEEDED ADMIRABLY IN GATHERING THE INFORMATION THE AGENDA NEEDS.
THE AUTHORITIES WILL FIND NO LINK TO US--ONLY A DISGRUNTLED LEXCORP EMPLOYEE WHO STOLE ONE OF MY EX-HUSBAND'S PROTOTYPES...
...A WIN-WIN SITUATION, TO MY MIND.
NOW, IT IS ESSENTIAL TO RETRIEVE SUPERMAN AND SUPERBOY TO CONTINUE OUR PLAN--TO GENETICALLY IMPROVE THE HUMAN RACE, MUCH AS WE DID YOU, GRAY LADY.
SO ESSENTIAL, EVERYONE ELSE IS EXPENDABLE.
EVERYONE.
SPECIAL AMMUNITION MARKED THE HEROES, SO THEY WILL BE SIMPLE TO TRACK WITH THE COMPUTER-NET IN GRAY LADY'S COSTUME.
THE PAIR ARE CLOSE BY, IN METROPOLIS, SO TAKE--
METROPOLIS?
BUT WHAT IF SOMEONE RECOGNIZES ME, CONTESSA? THAT'S WHERE I CAME FROM BEFORE YOU GAVE ME THESE WONDERFUL POWERS!
YOUR FAMILIARITY WITH THE CITY, IS EXACTLY WHY I WANT YOU LEADING THIS MISSION, YOUNG LADY.
THE CHANCE OF SEEING A FAMILIAR FACE IS NEARLY NON-EXISTENT...AND WOULDN'T ALTER MY PLANS, REGARDLESS
I'LL BE HOLDING MOST OF YOUR FELLOW POINT MEN IN RESERVE--BUT TAKE BLOCKADE WITH YOU...
...AND OUR OWN, IMPROVED CLONE OF SUPERBOY--MATCH!
WE WILL NOT FAIL YOU, CONTESSA. YOU HAVE MY WORD THE TWO METAS WILL NOT ESCAPE...

"...NOT ANYWHERE ON THIS WORLD."
GUARDS! REMOVE THIS GARBAGE...

...THIS PITIFUL EXCUSE FOR A MATE!
A SLAVE CAN KEEP A BED WARM-- BUT HE WHO SEEKS MAXIMA'S LOVE MUST BE EQUALLY SKILLED AT WAR!
ONLY SUPERMAN OF EARTH HAS PROVEN HIS WORTHINESS! HIS ONE FAULT IS HE DOES NOT REALIZE HOW PERFECTLY SUITED WE ARE FOR EACH OTHER!

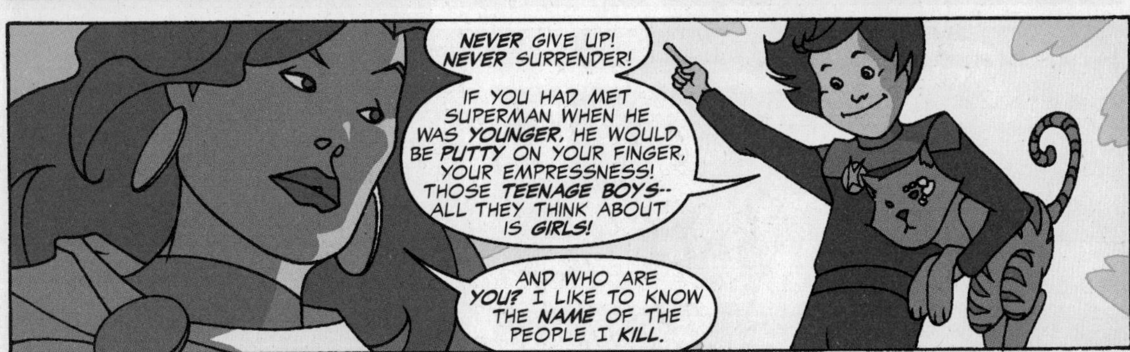
NEVER GIVE UP! NEVER SURRENDER!
IF YOU HAD MET SUPERMAN WHEN HE WAS YOUNGER, HE WOULD BE PUTTY ON YOUR FINGER, YOUR EMPRESSNESS! THOSE TEENAGE BOYS-- ALL THEY THINK ABOUT IS GIRLS!
AND WHO ARE YOU? I LIKE TO KNOW THE NAME OF THE PEOPLE I KILL.

ZZZAP
CALL ME KLARION-- BUM, BUM, BUM!-- THE WITCH BOY! AND YOU...

...I SHALL CALL YOU-- MINIMA!

THIS WILL NEVER WORK.
IT ALWAYS WORKS!
SO YOU AREN'T QUITE THE SAME AGE I AM...WAS...BUT LOIS WON'T NOTICE!
AFTER SHE KNOWS I'M OKAY--THEN WE'LL MAKE SURE THE AGENDA NEVER DOES TO ANYONE ELSE WHAT THEY DID TO TANA!
WHATEVER.
C'MON--TANA WAS YOUR FIRST LOVE! THIS HAS TO BE TEARING YOU UP INSIDE! THE SUPERBOY I KNOW WOULD BE READY TO TEAR UP THE AGENDA AS PAYBACK!
I KNOW IT'S WHAT I'D WANT TO DO!
WELL...ONE OF US HAS TO ACT LIKE AN ADULT.
I DON'T BUY THAT.
LISTEN--YOU CAN'T JUST IGNORE WHAT HAPPENED. YOU HAVE TO FACE IT...DEAL WITH IT...

LET'S WORRY ABOUT LOIS FIRST...
Bip Bop Bweep Boop Boop Boop Beep
LOIS LANE.
LOIS? LOIS, IT'S, UM...ME. YOU KNOW-- CLARK?
CONNECTION'S LOUSY, CLARK, AND TIME'S TIGHT--I HAVE A BIG INTERVIEW ON THE OTHER SIDE OF TOWN TO GET TO.
COULD YOU COME OVER TO THE WINDOW?
WON'T TAKE A MINUTE-- REALLY.
THERE! I SEE YOU!
OVER HERE! SEE ME?
YES. WHO'S WITH YOU?
WITH ME? UM, UHH...NO ONE, LOIS! IT'S JUST...ME!
HAD TO TELL YOU SOMETHING. SOMETHING VERY IMPORTANT...
BEEFBURGER ON A--
NO NO NO! BEEF BOURGUIGNON WITH KETCHUP! SHE KNOWS THAT MEANS I'M OKAY!
OH, I MEAN-- BEEF...BOOGER YAWN?
BOURGUIGNON! BOURGUIGNON! HAVE YOU EVER EATEN ANYWHERE BESIDES A FAST FOOD RESTAURANT?!

WHERE'S OLSEN? THIS HAS TO BE ONE OF HIS PRANKS.
I'M LEAVING NOW. IF ANYONE CALLS--TELL THEM I'M OUT INTERVIEWING THE FLASH.
THE REAL FLASH.
KLEP

HELLO? LOIS?
OH, GREAT! GIMME THAT! LEMME TALK!
LOIS, IT'S HARD TO HEAR YOU...

HONK
BEEP
VRRMM
EE-OO-EEE-OO
WOOGA
...THERE'S SO MUCH...

BEEP
THEY'RE ON THE OTHER SIDE OF THIS BUILDING! ATTACK!
...NOISE...
VRRMM
EE-OO-EEE-OO
WOOGA

KWOOOM

I GOT. SUPERBOY.
NO, BLOCKADE-- THAT'S SUPERMAN.
I THOUGHT YOU WERE TRACKING BOTH OF THEM, GRAY LADY.
GHRK--!
I WAS, MATCH.

THE OTHER ONE MUST BE NEARBY...
WITHIN EARSHOT--AND I DON'T MEAN THE SUPER-HEARING THAT TRIGGERED WHEN I WAS TRYING TO HEAR LOIS.
THAT'S GONE--BUT MATCH AND THE POINT MEN SURE AREN'T! IN HIS WEAKENED STATE, SUPERMAN DOESN'T STAND A CHANCE AGAINST THEM, SO...

...THIS LOOKS LIKE A JOB FOR SUPERBOY!

BET YOU THINK YOU'RE **STONE COLD**, DON'T YOU? WELL, THINGS ARE ABOUT TO **HEAT UP!**
YEAH--YOU'RE GOING OUT OF THE **FRYING PAN**, INTO THE **FIRE**, THANKS TO MY **HEAT VISION!**
ANY...ANY **SECOND** NOW! RIGHT **INTO** THE FIRE--!

I'M TIRED. OF WAITING.
KLUD
RECOGNIZE **ME**, MATCH? THE KID YOU ALWAYS **BEAT UP?** I'M ALL **GROWN UP** NOW, THANKS TO YOUR **BOSS!**
I THINK IT'S TIME WE ALL WORK THROUGH OUR **ISSUES!** YOU AND ME AND BLOCKADE AND GRAY LADY AND...

...**SUPERMAN?**

--YOU SAW SUPERMAN. GOOD. I MEAN, HE'S NO **BATMAN**, BUT...

BATMAN? BATMAN DOESN'T **EXIST!** HE'S AN **URBAN LEGEND!**

SUPERMAN'S **REAL!** I SAW **HIM!** HE'S--

UM...HE'S RIGHT OVER **THERE!**

SKRASH

YOU'RE NOT. GETTING AWAY. **THAT** EASY.

HEY, **BLOCKADE**-- THERE'S SOMEONE I WANT YOU TO **MEET...**

...THE **PAVEMENT!**

KRUNK

OH! THANK YOU VERY **MUCH!** I **NEVER** WOULD'VE THOUGHT OF DOING **THAT!**

DON'T YOU HAVE **YOUR OWN** VILLAIN TO FIGHT?

GIVE THE MAN OF STEEL A LITTLE **RESPECT,** KID! LEAVE IT TO YOU, HALF THE **BLOCK'D** GET DESTROYED!

CAN'T FIGURE WHY HE LETS YOU **WEAR** THAT S-SHIELD!

THANK GOD **SUPERMAN'S** HERE!

HE'LL **SAVE** US! HE ALWAYS **DOES!**

SUCH TRUST. HOW TOUCHING.
OF COURSE, YOU ARE THE ONE PLACING THEM IN DANGER. AFTER ALL, WE ONLY WANT YOU--AND YOUR YOUNG FRIEND.
RESISTANCE IS USELESS. EVEN IN YOUR MORE MATURE STATE, SUPERBOY, YOU ARE NO...MATCH FOR ME!

I AM YOUR GENETIC SUPERIOR, AND WILL ONE DAY TAKE YOUR PLACE...
...JUST AS THE AGENDA WILL ONE DAY REPLACE ALL MANKIND WITH A GENETICALLY SUPERIOR MASTER RACE.
IT IS INEVITABLE. IT IS THE NEW EVOLUTION.

IT'S WRONG!
YOU CAN'T REPLACE PEOPLE LIKE THEY'RE CLOTHES THAT WENT OUT OF STYLE!
YOU CAN'T TAKE MY PLACE--OR ANYONE'S PLACE! NO ONE CAN!
OH, YES. THIS FROM THE PERSON WHOSE ONE GOAL IS TO TAKE SUPERMAN'S PLACE.
I HEAR TANA MOON MET AN UNPLEASANT END. TELL ME--DID YOU WANT TO REPLACE HER WITH A CLONE? I WOULD HAVE, AND WE ARE SO MUCH ALIKE THAT--

I'M NOTHING LIKE YOU!
YOU DON'T EVEN DESERVE TO SAY TANA'S NAME!

FRZZA-KOOM

NO! DIDN'T...DIDN'T MEAN TO DO THAT!
CAN'T CONTROL MY HEAT VISION!
SUPERMAN--!

HE'S. BUSY. RIGHT NOW.
YEAH, WELL--STOP BEATING ON ME FOR A SECOND AND...AND THAT'LL CHANGE!

YOU THINK YOU ONLY HAVE TO WORRY ABOUT BLOCKADE? HIS BLOWS MUST'VE LEFT YOU MORE ADDLED THAN I HOPED!

DON'T WORRY-- THIS'LL BE OVER...

THWANNG
...BEFORE YOU KNOW WHAT HIT YOU!

OKAY... MAYBE...
...MAYBE I DON'T HAVE ENOUGH POWER TO STOP YOU TWO ON MY OWN, SO...I GUESS I'LL HAVE TO...

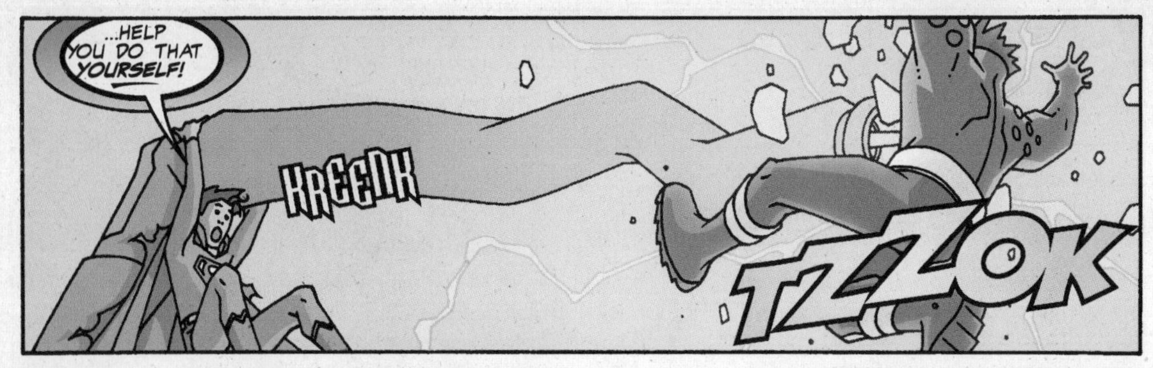
...HELP YOU DO THAT YOURSELF!
KREENK
TZZOK

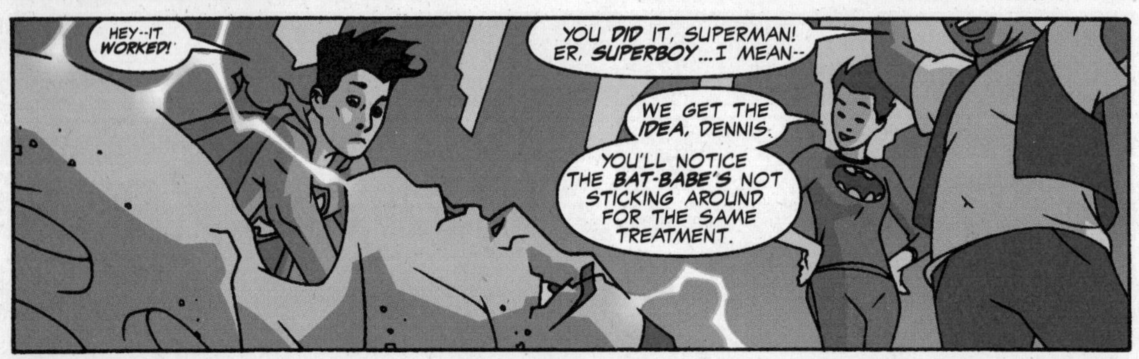
HEY--IT WORKED!
YOU DID IT, SUPERMAN! ER, SUPERBOY...I MEAN--
WE GET THE IDEA, DENNIS.
YOU'LL NOTICE THE BAT-BABE'S NOT STICKING AROUND FOR THE SAME TREATMENT.

WHAT--?
I KNOW THOSE VOICES! IT CAN'T BE--!

HUH--!?
WHUNK
NNF--!

FZZZAKOOM

IT STOPPED! THE HEAT VISION STOPPED!
NOT SOON ENOUGH!
HURM...?
IS THAT. A BUILDING. FALLING?

BIG CHUNK OF IT! DON'T JUST STAND THERE!
SAME FOR YOU TWO!
SUPERBOY-- CATCH!

WHOOM
SUPERMAN--!

MY GOD! BLOCKADE MIGHT HAVE SURVIVED THAT--BUT SUPERMAN...?
NO! IT WON'T HAPPEN AGAIN! NOT AFTER WHAT HAPPENED TO TANA--!
GOT TO FIND HIM-- QUICKLY! BUT THIS RUBBLE--IF ONLY I COULD JUST...

...MOVE IT ALL...?

OF COURSE!
NOT ONLY DID I GET NEW POWERS AS AN ADULT--MY TACTILE-TELEKINESIS HAS INCREASED...EXPANDED!
TIME FOR THAT LATER! WHERE'S SUPERMAN--?

DOWN... HERE...
LUCK...LUCKILY, BLOCKADE ABSORBED THE CRASH...
ERHM...MOST OF THE CRASH...
LOOK, COULD YOU...GET RID OF THOSE ROCKS? REALLY HATE TO HAVE THEM...FALL ON ME AGAIN...
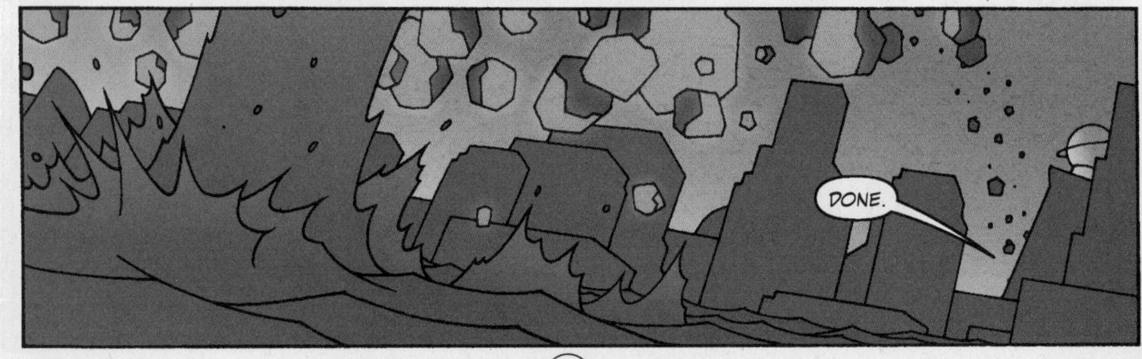
DONE.

OKAY... I'M OKAY NOW...
NEVER...NEVER REALIZED HOW HARD IT IS BEING SUPERBOY...EVERYONE EXPECTING YOU TO BE SUPERMAN...
NEWSFLASH--IT'S NOT EXACTLY CAKE BEING SUPERMAN, EITHER. ALL THAT POWER, ALL THAT RESPONSIBILITY, NO ROOM FOR MISTAKES...
DO YOU NEED--?
STAY AWAY!
SH'YEAH! LIKE HE'S GOTTA TELL US TWICE!

MISTAKES? I...I'VE MADE MY SHARE. LIKE NOT TELLING YOU MY...SECRETS.
DIDN'T...PARTLY BECAUSE I WANTED...MY PRIVACY...BUT ALSO BECAUSE IT WOULD'VE FELT ALMOST LIKE I WAS TRAINING...MY REPLACEMENT.
COULDN'T DO THAT...COULDN'T ADMIT I'D EVER NEED ONE. I WAS WRONG...
NO. NO ONE WILL EVER REPLACE YOU--LEAST OF ALL ME.
I'M PROUD TO WEAR THE S-SHIELD, AND WILL ALWAYS TRY TO LIVE UP TO IT--BUT I'LL DO THAT BY MAKING THE NAME SUPERBOY MEAN AS MUCH AS SUPERMAN DOES.

STARTING NOW...
UGHHH...
ALL RIGHT, GRAY LADY--THIS IS THE DEAL. THE ONLY DEAL.
THE AUTHORITIES WILL BE HERE SOON. THEY'LL PLACE MATCH AND BLOCKADE IN CUSTODY.

SUPERMAN'S HURT--HOW BAD, I DON'T KNOW--BUT I WON'T TAKE HIM ANYWHERE THE AGENDA WILL ATTACK AGAIN AND PUT EVEN MORE LIVES AT RISK.
I ASSUME THE AGENDA HAS ITS OWN FACILITIES, ADVANCED ENOUGH TO CARE FOR SUPERMAN?
ABSOLUTELY. I'LL SEE TO IT HE GETS THE BEST CARE POSSIBLE.

THEN WE SURRENDER.

WILL YOU BOYS PLEASE--
--STOP--
--FIGHTING!
Coming of Age
Written by BRIAN K. VAUGHAN
Pencilled by SCOTT KOLINS
Inked by CHRIS IVY
Colored by RICK TAYLOR
Lettered by KEN LOPEZ
Edited by MAUREEN McTIGUE
WONDER WOMAN created by WILLIAM MOULTON MARSTON

YOUNG LADY, PUT THOSE DOWN THIS INSTANT!
DON'T BE SO CONDESCENDING, CASSIE. THAT WITCH BOY KLARION MAY HAVE MADE ME LOOK YOUNGER, BUT I'M STILL MATURE ENOUGH TO BELIEVE IN MY MISSION OF PEACE.
MATURE? DIANA, YOU'VE BEEN ACTING BRASH, HEADSTRONG AND RECKLESS!
THIS ISN'T EVEN A REAL BATTLE! THESE ARE JUST SOLDIERS PLAYING WAR GAMES!
OH.
WELL... WAR IS NOT A GAME. AND I... I DEMAND TO SPEAK TO THE MAN RESPONSIBLE FOR THIS MESS!
DIANA, NO!

SHE'S COMING RIGHT AT US!
WHAT IN THE SAM HILL...?
WONDER WOMAN!
RUN FOR YOUR LIVES!
YES?
I DON'T KNOW WHAT THIS IS ALL ABOUT, MA'AM, BUT YOU'RE JUST LUCKY THOSE WERE DECOMMISSIONED SCRAP TANKS.
IF WE'D BEEN PRACTICING WITH REAL M-1'S, YOUR LITTLE GIRL WOULD HAVE OWED THE TAXPAYERS MUCH MORE THAN HER ALLOWANCE COULD AFFORD.
I AM NOT HER-- =MMMPH=!
I'M SO SORRY, GENERAL. I ASSURE YOU THAT SHE'LL BE... UM, GROUNDED FOR CAUSING YOU ALL THIS TROUBLE. WE'LL JUST, UH, BE ON OUR WAY. THANKS. 'BYE, NOW.
HOLY... WHEN DID WONDER WOMAN GO BLONDE?
WHO CARES? LOOK AT THOSE WONDER GAMS!
THAT'S IT. WE'RE GOING HOME AND CHANGING CLOTHES NOW. HOW DO YOU PUT UP WITH WEARING THIS OUTFIT, DIANA?
I HAVE NO IDEA WHAT YOU MEAN. AND BESIDES, IT WAS YOUR IDEA TO TRADE COSTUMES.
YEAH, WELL, YOU DON'T EXACTLY FILL OUT THIS THING.
HMPH. NOR DO YOU, I MIGHT ADD.
=SIGH= YOU MUST HAVE BEEN SOME HANDFUL WHEN YOU WERE A KID...

GOOD LORD! COULD THIS REALLY BE--
--MY ROOM?!
DIANA, AM I HONESTLY SO... SO--
YOUNG? YES. YES, YOU ARE.
BUT HOW COULD ONE GIRL HAVE SO MANY "TITANIC" POSTERS? I JUST CAN'T BELIEVE THAT A FEW HOURS AGO I WAS THIS PERSON!
CASSIE, THESE FEELINGS ARE ONLY NATURAL.
WELL... AS NATURAL AS ANYONE CAN FEEL AFTER SOME KIND OF BLAST MADE THEM FIFTEEN YEARS OLDER, I GUESS.
THE POINT IS THAT YOU'RE GROWN-UP NOW, AND WITH ADULTHOOD OFTEN COME MATURITY, PERSPECTIVE AND CONFIDENCE.
TRUST ME, I SHOULD KNOW.
OH, OF COURSE, YOUR WORSHIPNESS...
STILL, YOU'RE RIGHT ABOUT ONE THING. I AM OLDER NOW--
--SO MAYBE THE TIME HAS FINALLY COME--

--TO WEAR THIS!
OH MY GODDESS!
I NEVER IMAGINED HOW GREAT DONNA TROY'S ATTIRE WOULD LOOK ON YOU, CASSIE!
I DON'T KNOW. I DIDN'T REALLY EARN THE RIGHT TO WEAR THIS. PUTTING IT ON NOW KIND OF FEELS LIKE CHEATING.
DON'T BE SILLY! YOU HAVE EVERY RIGHT TO FEEL COMFORTABLE WEARING DONNA'S COLORS TO BATTLE.
SPEAKING OF COMFORT, THESE STUPID GOGGLES COULD CUT OFF THE CIRCULATION TO EVEN ATHENA'S MIGHTY BRAIN. MAYBE I SHOULD FIND A DIFFERENT GETUP, TOO.
TAKE WHATEVER YOU WANT, DIANA. I THINK I'VE GOT A CARDIGAN THAT MIGHT FIT YOU.
I'M GOING TO TRY TO FIND DONNA'S BOOTS DOWNSTAIRS. JUST HOLLER IF YOU NEED--
--HELP?

WHO THE HELL ARE YOU, AND WHAT WERE YOU DOING IN MY DAUGHTER'S ROOM?
MOM?!
I DIDN'T EVEN KNOW YOU WERE HOME. IT'S ME! IT'S CASSIE!
NO. YOU'RE NOT...
CASSIE! BABY, I THOUGHT THOSE GOVERNMENT PEOPLE KILLED YOU!
THE NEWS SAID YOU WERE DANGEROUS... OUT OF CONTROL! I WAS AFRAID YOU WERE DEAD!
MOM, THOSE STORIES ARE LIES! I'M FINE! REALLY! WHY ARE YOU CRYING?
MY LITTLE BABY, YOU'RE ALL...YOU'RE ALL GROWN UP.
CASSANDRA, WHAT HAPPENED?

MOM, I'M NOT A KID ANYMORE. I WASN'T EVEN A "KID" WHEN I WAS STILL A TEENAGER! I MEAN, THIS WHOLE EXPERIENCE HAS TAUGHT ME A LOT ABOUT MYSELF...

DO YOU HONESTLY THINK ROBIN IS SITTING AT HOME HAVING A HEART-TO HEART WITH HIS PARENTS? HE NEVER DOUBTS HIMSELF, NEVER WORRIES ABOUT WHAT MIGHT GO WRONG.

HE'S A HERO, AND NOW MORE THAN EVER, I REALIZE THAT THAT'S WHAT I WANT TO BE... WHAT I AM.

I...I SUPPOSE I'VE ALWAYS KNOWN THAT, BUT IT'S NOT GOING TO BE EASY FOR ME. YOU'RE STILL MY LITTLE GIRL, CASSIE. I WORRY ABOUT YOU.

WELL, SOMETIMES I WORRY ABOUT YOU, MOM. LIKE RIGHT NOW! WHERE IN THE WORLD DID YOU EVER GET A GUN?

SPLOOSH

IN YOUR TOY BOX.

MISS GROWN-UP...

I PROMISE THAT MY FIRST PRIORITY IS MAKING EVERYTHING THE WAY IT WAS, MOM. I'M GOING TO BE YOUR TEENAGER AGAIN...
BUT AS LONG AS I'M AN ADULT, I JUST WANTED TO LET YOU KNOW THAT I FINALLY UNDERSTAND HOW HARD IT MUST BE TO HAVE ME FOR A DAUGHTER.
FOR THE PAST FEW HOURS, I'VE HAD TO CLEAN UP AFTER MY OWN--
--WONDER BRAT?
HELLO, HELENA. I WISH WE HAD MORE TIME FOR CHITCHAT, BUT YOUR DAUGHTER AND I HAVE WORK TO DO.
THERE'S ONLY ONE MAN WHO CAN ALTER THE VERY AGES OF AMAZONS AND MORTALS ALIKE.
LADIES, IT'S TIME WE PAY A VISIT... TO ZEUS!

PARKING
CITY of GATEWAY DEPT. of TRAFFIC
UH, CORRECT ME IF I'M WRONG, BUT IT'S NOT REALLY POSSIBLE TO GET TO MOUNT OLYMPUS VIA MINIVAN.
WELL, CASSIE, RIGHT NOW I'M MUCH TOO WEAK TO BREAK THROUGH THE MYSTIC REALMS ON MY OWN.
THANKFULLY FOR ME, WHEN I WORKED AT YOUR MOM'S MUSEUM, I CAME ACROSS AN ANCIENT DEVICE THAT MORTALS ONCE USED TO CONTACT THE GODS.
WITH HELENA'S HELP, WE'RE GOING TO FIX THAT MACHINE AND PUT IN A CALL TO ZEUS.
CASSIE, BE CAREFUL!
IF THE MYSTIC POOL OVERFLOWS, YOU'LL RELEASE HELLHOUNDS FROM HADES INTO OUR WORLD!
TAKE IT EASY, MOM. I CAN DO THIS...
STAND BACK, HELENA. THE POWER FROM MY MAGIC LASSO SHOULD BE ABLE TO JUMPSTART THIS THING...
NOW HOW DOES THAT CHANT GO?
UM...HEAR ME, MY KING! O LORD OF THE...UM, HEAVENS, SON OF CRONUS AND... WELL, YOU KNOW. ANSWER MY CRIES! PLEASE?
WHO DARES ADDRESS THIS GOD?!
OKAY, THAT DIDN'T SOUND LIKE ZEUS...
UH-OH.

I AM APOLLO, GOD OF LIGHT, BROTHER OF ARTEMIS AND SON OF MIGHTY ZEUS.
WHY IN THE NAME OF CERBERUS DOES SOMEONE FROM YOUR LOWLY REALM THINK THEMSELVES WORTHY TO SEEK MY AUDIENCE?
PRETTY GRUMPY FOR A "GOD OF LIGHT."
DIANA!
SORRY. UM, GREAT APOLLO, I KNOW I DON'T EXACTLY LOOK LIKE THE PRINCESS OF THEMYSCIRA, BUT I SWEAR IT'S ME... DIANA!
YOU KNOW, I SAT WITH YOU AS GODDESS OF TRUTH FOR A BIT.
RING ANY BELLS?
ANYWAY, WE'RE ACTUALLY LOOKING FOR ZEUS, SO IF YOU COULD JUST PUT HIM ON THE LINE, WE'D REALLY--
MY FATHER IS OFF FRATERNIZING WITH MORTALS AT THE MOMENT.
WHILE THAT MAY BE HIS WONT, IT IS CERTAINLY NOT MINE. BE GONE, AMAZON. I WILL HAVE NOTHING MORE TO DO WITH YOU...
APOLLO, WAIT!
CASSIE, NO!

AND WHO IS THIS IMPUDENT SLATTERN?
THE NAME IS CASSANDRA SANDSMARK. YOUR FATHER GRANTED ME POWERS BECAUSE HE RESPECTED ME. I'M HOPING THAT COUNTS FOR SOMETHING WITH YOU.
DIANA AND I JUST NEED TO BE RESTORED TO OUR RIGHTFUL AGES. THAT'S ALL WE ASK OF YOU.
PLEASE.
CASSANDRA, EH? I HAVE HEARD OF YOU.
SADLY, UNLIKE MY DODDERING FATHER, I AM NOT IN THE HABIT OF SIMPLY GIVING THINGS TO UNDESERVING LITTLE MORTALS.
STILL, YOUR BOLDNESS AMUSES ME. I SHALL HELP YOU... IF YOU MEET MY CHALLENGE.
BEFORE SHE WAS KILLED BY PERSEUS, THE GORGON SISTER MEDUSA MATED WITH POLYPHEMUS, THE CYCLOPS BLINDED BY ODYSSEUS.
THEY SIRED A MONSTER NAMED CYCLON. TO THIS DAY, THE BEAST HAS RESIDED UNCHALLENGED ON AN ISLAND IN THE AEGEAN SEA. CYCLON HAS A HELMET THAT ONCE BELONGED TO ME. I WANT IT BACK.
IF YOU TWO RETRIEVE THIS BOON FOR ME, I SHALL REPAIR THE MYSTICAL DAMAGE DONE TO YOUR BODIES... BUT ONLY IF YOU ACCOMPLISH THIS TASK BEFORE THE SUN RISES!
UNTIL THEN, MORTAL.
CASSIE, I WON'T LET YOU! YOU CAN'T PLAY GAMES WITH JEALOUS GODS! IT'S SUICIDE!
I'M SORRY, MOM. WHAT CHOICE DO I HAVE? LET'S GO, DIANA.
THE CYCLON. WHY'D IT HAVE TO BE THE CYCLON?

I WONDER WHAT ADVENTURE OUR PRINCESS EMBARKS UPON THIS EVENING?
DIANA HAS NOT BEEN TO THE WONDERDOME IN SOME TIME. I PRAY THE GODS HAVE BEEN WITH HER...
TELL ME, CHIRON... WHAT HAS THE BODY OF A CHILD, THE POWERS OF A WIZARD, AND THE CUNNING OF A DEVIL?
DAMNATION, SPHINX, YOUR PROPHESYING RIDDLES ALWAYS CONFOUND ME. PRAY TELL, WHAT IS THE ANSWER?
ME!
I AM KLARION... BUM, BUM, BUM... THE WITCH BOY, CENTAUR, AND I HAVE COME TO TURN WONDER WOMAN'S MOST TRUSTED SPHINX INTO AN IMPRESSIONABLE CHILD, SO THAT I MAY USE HER AGAINST YOUR PRINCESS!
ZAPPY
ZAPPY
SPHINX, DO NOT GIVE IN TO THIS WARLOCK!
KNOCK KNOCK...
SPHINX, I DO NOT UNDERSTAND! "KNOCK KNOCK"? WHY... WHO IS THERE?
PASTURE!
PASTURE WHO, SPHINX?
PASTURE BEDTIME, NO?
POW
BRILLIANT, MY INFANT MINION!
NOW COME, WE HAVE MAYHEM TO SPREAD...

CASSIE, WE'LL NEVER GET THAT HELMET BEFORE SUNRISE!
YOU KNOW, THE YOUNGER YOU IS A REAL PESSIMIST.
NO, JUST A REALIST, CASSIE.
DO YOU HAVE ANY IDEA HOW MANY HEROES THE GODS SENT TO THEIR DEATHS ON QUESTS JUST LIKE THIS ONE? DO YOU KNOW WHAT A MONSTER LIKE MEDUSA IS CAPABLE OF?
SURE, I SAW "CLASH OF THE TITANS" A DOZEN TIMES. YOU CAN TURN TO STONE JUST BY LOOKING AT MEDUSA, RIGHT?
YES, AND HER CHILD HAS THAT SAME POWER, NOT TO MENTION THE STRENGTH AND SIZE OF A CYCLOPS!
DON'T TAKE THIS LIGHTLY, CASSIE. THIS MAY VERY WELL BE THE GREATEST CHALLENGE OF YOUR LIFE. YOU HAVE TO FIGHT THIS CREATURE WITH EVERYTHING YOU HAVE. IF YOU LET UP FOR EVEN A MOMENT, YOU'RE AS GOOD AS DEAD.
IT'S NOT TOO LATE TO TURN BACK IF YOU'RE FRIGHTENED, YOU KNOW...
NO... I'M I'M READY FOR THIS. I HAVE TO BE A HERO. I--
WAIT... DID YOU HEAR SOMETHING?

RRRRRARRGH!
FOR THE LOVE OF HESTIA... LOOK AWAY!

HOW ARE WE SUPPOSED TO FIGHT SOMETHING THAT WE'RE NOT ALLOWED TO SEE?
HASN'T ARTEMIS TAUGHT YOU ANYTHING?
"WHEN A WARRIOR CANNOT USE HER EYES, SHE MUST RELY ON HER OTHER SENSES!"
THWACK

LISTEN FOR THE CREATURE'S BREATH AND--
OONF!
WELL, MY SENSES TELL ME THAT DIDN'T SOUND GOOD...

SPLOOSH
I GUESS IT'S NOW OR NEVER...
LET'S DANCE, YOU BIG, UGLY--
CHOMP
SPNISH
FWOOOSH
UNN--
--UNF!
OKAY, I DON'T KNOW WHAT JUST HAPPENED, BUT I DO NOT LIKE HOW IT SMELLS...

CASSIE, THAT THING JUST KNOCKED ME HALFWAY ACROSS **GREECE**! WHAT ARE WE SUPPOSED TO **DO**?

DON'T **PANIC**! I'LL DISTRACT HIM WHILE YOU TIE YOUR **LASSO** AROUND HIS **FEET**! THE BIGGER THEY ARE--

--THE FLATTER THEY **SQUASH**!

CASSIE, THIS IS NEVER GOING TO **WORK**! HE'S WAY TOO STRONG TO **FIGHT**!

<YOU... YOU SPEAK MY ***TONGUE?***>

<***BROTHER...*** WE MEAN YOU... ***NO HARM!***>*

* TRANSLATED FROM THE ANCIENT GREEK.

<FORGIVE THIS ***MISUNDERSTANDING,*** MY ***FRIENDS!*** I WAS MERELY DEFENDING MY ***HOME!***>

<YOU ARE MOST ***WELCOME*** HERE!>

I HAVE NO IDEA WHAT YOU JUST ***SAID...*** BUT IT SURE SOUNDED ***GOOD!***

IT'S SAFE TO LOOK AT HIM, CASSIE!
CYCLON WAS JUST TELLING ME HOW HIS PARENTS FORCED HIM OUT OF THEIR HOUSE BECAUSE THEY WERE DISAPPOINTED HOW GENTLE AND HARMLESS HE WAS.
I GUESS EVERY KID HAS TROUBLE LIVING UP TO ADULTS' EXPECTATIONS, HUH?
WE THANK YOU FOR YOUR KINDNESS, CYCLON. YOU HAVE NO IDEA HOW MUCH THIS HELMET MEANS TO US.
CYCLON SAID THAT APOLLO GAVE HIM THAT GIFT AGES AGO AND INSTRUCTED HIM TO RELEASE IT TO PEOPLE WHO ASKED FOR IT... BUT TO KILL THOSE WHO FOUGHT FOR IT.
I DON'T TRUST ZEUS' SON, CASSIE. WE SHOULD GIVE APOLLO HIS LOUSY HELMET AND BE DONE WITH HIM.
NO ARGUMENTS THERE.
<THANK YOU SO MUCH FOR YOUR HOSPITALITY, CYCLON, BUT I'M AFRAID WE REALLY HAVE TO GET GOING.>
<THANK YOU FOR YOUR COMPANY, PRINCESS. I WISH YOU LUCK WITH YOUR ODYSSEY!>
CASSIE...I'M SORRY ABOUT MY BEHAVIOR TODAY. REALLY. I HAD FORGOTTEN HOW HARD IT IS TO BE YOUNG, AND I'M MORE PROUD THAN EVER OF WHAT YOU HAVE DONE WITH YOUR YEARS. I--
DIANA... LOOK!

WONDER GIRL, THIS IS THE UNITED STATES GOVERNMENT ORDERING YOU TO SURRENDER YOURSELF TO US IMMEDIATELY!
THERE'S NO POINT IN FIGHTING! WE HAVE ALREADY TAKEN SUPERBOY INTO CUSTODY...
KON...

WE RECEIVED AN ANONYMOUS TIP THAT YOU AND A COMPANION WOULD BE ON THIS ISLAND. GIVE YOURSELVES UP NOW!

HA HA HA HA HA HA HA!

CASSIE, YOU KNOW THOSE MEN AREN'T FROM THE GOVERNMENT. THEY'RE AGENDA'S SOLDIERS! WE CAN TAKE THEM DOWN IN A SECOND!

YES...BUT WE'RE NOT GOING TO FIGHT, DIANA. WE'RE GOING TO GIVE OURSELVES UP.

ARE YOU INSANE?

WHAT ABOUT APOLLO'S CHALLENGE? IF WE DON'T GET THIS HELMET BACK TO HIM SOON, WE COULD BE STUCK LIKE THIS FOREVER!

THAT'S A RISK WE'LL HAVE TO TAKE.

THIS COULD BE OUR ONLY CHANCE TO FIND AND RESCUE SUPERBOY. I DON'T WANT TO BE A GROWN UP ANY MORE THAN YOU WANT TO BE A TEENAGER--

--BUT I REFUSE TO ABANDON ONE OF MY TEAMMATES.

IF YOU SAY SO, CASSIE... BUT I PRAY TO HERA YOUR TROJAN HORSE DOESN'T GET US KILLED!

SOMEWHERE, IN THE LUNATIC SKIES ABOVE CHEVY CHASE, MARYLAND...
Come ON, Deadboy! We don't have time for this!!
We have to focus on finding KLARION and finding a way to get him to reverse this spell! Not wasting our time dealing with a... a bunch of KIDS!!
BUT... THAT'S! NOT! FAIR!!
WISPY RIBBONS OF SWIRLING SMOKE TWIST AND TWIRL ABOUT THE YOUNG WOMAN CALLED THE SECRET, UNCONSCIOUSLY TAPPING INTO HER SUBCONSCIOUS, COALESCING FOR BUT A MOMENT--
--INTO AN IMAGE OF HOW THINGS SHOULD BE...
THAT IS, OF COURSE, IF THE WORLD HADN'T RECENTLY GONE--

--COMPLETELY NUTS!!
HOT ON THE HEELS OF REJUVENATING AND/OR AGING VARIOUS MEMBERS OF THE
YOUNG JUSTICE
THE DEVILISH IMP KNOWN AS KLARION... BUM BUM BUM... THE WITCH BOY, HAS ABSCONDED INTO THE SUBURBS SURROUNDING WASHINGTON, D.C.--
--TURNING THESE QUAINT AND QUIET COMMUNITIES INTO MODELS OF MAYHEM AND MADNESS WITH HIS MIRTHFUL MAGIC!
HERE, THE WORLD HAS TURNED UPSIDE-DOWN AS INANIMATE OBJECTS COME TO LIFE AND NONSENSE RULES!!
AND YET, EVEN IN THE FACE OF A WORLD GONE AWRY...
...SOME THINGS NEVER CHANGE...
SO WHAT?! WHADDA YOU GONNA DO ABOUT IT...?!
CHEVY CHASE CHAMPS

"Looking for Trouble..."
todd dezago wrote it! • michael avon oeming drew it!
jason baumgartner inked it! • bill oakley lettered it!
pat garrahy colored it! • digital chameleon separated it!
maureen mctigue associated it! • eddie berganza eddied it!
CC
POLICE

LISTEN, "BUFFY"-- OR WHATEVER YOUR NAME IS... YOU'RE JUST NOT GETTIN' IT, ARE YA...?
No! Come on! We weren't sent out here to--
EVEN THOUGH THAT KLARION CREEP TURNED ME INTO A MINI-ME VERSION OF MY FORMER GHOSTLY SELF...
... I'M STILL AN AGENT OF KARMIC JUSTICE! IT'S MY JOB TO BALANCE THE SCALES OF RIGHT AND WRONG...
...AND THAT'S NOT FAIR!!
CUT IT OUT, NELSON! GIVE RYAN HIS BOARD BACK!
YOU'RE JUST JEALOUS 'CAUSE HE'S A BETTER BOARDER THAN YOU!
SHUT UP, WUSS! IT'S MY RAMP--
--AND I'LL DECIDE WHO CAN AND CAN'T SKATE HERE!
HA!
KRAK
HEY!
YOU... YOU BROKE RYAN'S BOARD!

THAT CUTS IT! THIS KID'S GONNA PAY BIG TIME!
HAW-HAW! WHADDAYA GONNA DO ABOUT IT, YA BUNCHA LOS--
SHPRAKT!
--ZOINK!
Oh, this isn't good...

GEE, YOU GUYS... I'M SORRY!
Y'SEE, I'M JUST A BIG IGNORAMUS WITH LOW SELF-ESTEEM WHO USES MY 'HUSKY' SIZE TO MY ADVANTAGE, LORDING OVER THOSE SMALLER THAN ME AND INTIMIDATING THEM WITH FEAR.
I APOLOGIZE FOR BUSTIN' YOUR BOARD, RYAN. HERE--TAKE ALL THE MONEY I HAVE IN MY POCKETS...
AND HERE'S MY CLOTHES, TOO!

AND TAKE MY SKATEBOARD, TOO! I WANTCHA TO HAVE IT! 'CAUSE I'M SUCH A JERK.

HEY! PAINT! I GOT AN IDEA...
Umm, ELIZABETH, YOU ARE GETTIN' ALLA THIS ON TAPE, RIGHT...?

HOW'S THAT? I WANT EVERYONE TO KNOW!
NELSON IS A IDIOT

I'M A DOPE! AND A BULLY! AND I CRIED DURING "POXY MONSTERS"!
CHEVY CHASE CHAMP
NELSON IS A IDIOT

Heh-heh! THAT OUGHTA DO IT...

YOU'RE ON YOUR OWN, NELSON...
...AND SOMETIMES I HAVE BAD DREAMS ABOUT WALKING DOWN THE STREET IN MY...

URK!
HEY... HOW DID I--?
WHAT--
--WHAT HAPPENED?!
NELSON IS A IDIOT

OH... ummm...
...NOTHING.
SKATER

BWA-HA-HA-HA!!
SKATERS

yipe!
HAHAHAHA HA!
...AND I'M TELLING YOU! WALK!
BUT... BUT... BUT...
SO, BOSS... WHADDAWE DO NOW?
BOSS?! ME?!? I'M not in charge! I'm... I'm...
...I'm just a kid!
NO, I'M JUST A KID! YOU'RE THE ADULT HERE NOW, SO THAT MAKES YOU THE LEADER!
BESIDES, YOU CAN FOLLOW KLARION'S WITCH-MAGIC TRAIL BETTER THAN I CAN...
sigh
Okay, then if I'm in charge, that means you've gotta start listening to me...
...no more running off impulsively... I've got plenty of that back in Young Justice...
Klarion's responsible for you getting younger and me getting older-- along with all the others--
--and since you and I are the only ones who can 'see' his residual magical energy trail--
--we have the most important job of finding him and getting him to reverse this stupid spell! 'Cause if we don't--
--WE'LL BE STUCK LIKE THIS FOREVER...!
SO LET'S GO GET KLARION!

MEANWHILE, ELSEWHERE...
STEP RIGHT UP! RIGHT THIS WAY, YOU RECENTLY REJUVENATED RASCALS!!
I MEAN, AFTER MAKING ALL THOSE PAIN-IN-THE-BUTT GROWN-UP STUPIDHEROES INTO KIDS AGAIN, I THOUGHT IT'D BE ONLY FAIR--
--TO GIVE THEM A GANG OF MINI-BAD GUYS TO KEEP THEM BUSY!!
--AND LOTS OF FUN!!--
SO COME ON IN!! ENJOY THE CIRCUS!! IT'S THE GREATEST, MOST FABULOUS SHOW ON EARTH!!
LADEEEEZ AAAND GENTLEMEN! AND CHILLLDREN OF ALLLLL AGES!! WELLCOME TO--
AND THAT SHOULD KEEP ALLA YOU RUG-RATS ENTERTAINED WHILE I GO SEE WHAT OTHER CHAOS I CAN CAUSE!

SO THAT'S IT?! WE JUST FOLLOW THE ENERGY TRAIL UNTIL WE CATCH UP TO KLARION?!
I...I guess so...I've never done this before, but I suppose--
THEN WHADDA WE WAITIN' FOR?!--
LET'S GO GET 'ETHEREAL' ON HIS BUTT!
Deadboy! WAIT! Don't--
My God, he's just like Impulse...
...or is that just the way it is with all kids...? Am I that way...? Or am I just noticing this NOW 'cause I'm...
...an adult...?
And...in charge...?
C'MON, YA SLUG! LET'S GO!
Help!

JEEZ, LOUISE!!
LISTEN, SECRET--I KNOW YOU SAID WE GOTTA CONCENTRATE ON CATCHIN' UP TO THE WITCH BOY, BUT WE HAFTA DO SOMETHIN' ABOUT THIS TRAIL OF CHAOS HE'S LEFT BEHIND--
...I MEAN, THIS IS INSANE!!
♪ hmm hmm hmmmm ♪
BLART!
YIIEEE!
BLARFF!
MOMMA!
Just try to relax, sir--let the smoke lift you.
TH-THANK YOU! BUT WHAT...
...WHAT'S GOING ON?!?
FOOOOSHH!

"Just a bit of rampant Madness... We're, umm, we're working on it..."
BLARRRR!
RAAHHHR!
ARCADE
RUN!
AAHHH!

THIS IS WACKED!
EVERYTHING'S GOIN' CRAZY! EVERYTHING'S COMING TO LIFE!
AND NOW, INSTEADA THOSE KIDS TRYIN' TO BEAT THE VIDEO GAMES...

ARCADE
BZZT
"...THE VIDEO GAMES ARE BEATING THEM!"

WELL, IF MACHINES CAN COME TO 'LIFE,' THEN I CAN POSSESS 'EM! LET'S SEE HOW THEY LIKE A TASTE--
SODA

--OF THEIR OWN MEDICINE!
SODA
SODA
ARRGH!
YIPE! YIPE!

AND, SHORTLY...
Klarion's trail doesn't stretch on much further--
--he has to be right around here somewh--
HOLY CATS!! ALL THIS TIME WE HAVEN'T BEEN FOLLOWIN' KLARION AT ALL...!
IT'S THAT STUPID CAT OF HIS, TEEKL!!
WE'VE BEEN DECKED!
HSSSS!

WELL, THEN, CALL ME 'CURIOSITY,' 'CAUSE I'M GONNA KILL THAT CA--
MRROWWR!
POOF!
KRA-POW!
Deadboy! Wait!
Teekl is Klarion's 'familiar'-- his conduit to the magic he uses--she's magical, too!
SORRY. I KNEW THAT!...I'M JUST NOT THINKING TOO CLEARLY IN THIS LITTLE DEAD BODY...
I'M TRYIN' TO LISTEN--BUT IT'S HARD...
That's okay. I think we can still track her...
As long as Teekl left a puff of smoke like this one wherever she reappeared--
--I should be able to 'smoke-jump' us there and maybe catch her by surprise! Maybe Klarion, too...
POOF!
FWOOOSH!
HEY! I FEEL LIKE A MILKSHAKE!

This... is where she went?! To a--
POOOF!
DOLLMIKE
A CIRCUS!
Deadboy! There she is! We've got to--
THIS IS IT! THIS IS WHAT I LIVED FOR!! WELL, WHEN I LIVED...!
THE ROAR OF THE GREASEPAINT, THE SMELL OF THE CROWD...!
THE HIGH WIRE WAS MY LIFE! I COULDA BEEN THE GREATEST AERIALIST OF ALL TIME!
IF NOT FOR THAT STUPID ASSASSIN'S BULLET...
OH, I AM SO NOT GONNA MISS AN OPPORTUNITY LIKE THIS!
RINGO BROS. CIRCUS
... HIGH ABOVE THE CENTER RING, LADIES AND GENTLEMEN, AS THE ZUCCHINI FAMILY WILL ATTEMPT A STUNT NOT DARED SINCE THE LEGENDARY FLYING GRAYSONS PERFORMED IT NEARLY TEN YEARS AGO...

GIMME A TICKET! I'M IN!
WHILE, BELOW--
SO much for my 'partner'-- lost him again! He's being such a... kid!
But I've gotta stay after Teekl...
I can't let her get away this time! She has to lead us to--
STORAGE NO ADMITTANCE
Huh?! What's she up to now?
She's just sitting there, smiling up at me... maybe Deadboy was right!...
Maybe she's just playing decoy-- setting me up for Klarion's amb--
AAAAAAAA--
WHAM!
HEE HEE HEE! EXCELLENT, MY PRECIOUS... EXCELLENT!
?
THUMP!

NO! NOOOO! Let me--
SHE FEELS THE PANIC ENGULF HER IMMEDIATELY--SENSES THE TIGHTNESS OF THE COFFIN CLOSING IN AROUND HER--THE STYGIAN DARKNESS...CLUTCHING AT HER--
--ENCIRCLING HER--
--TRYING TO SMOTHER HER LIGHT AND WISPY FORM IN ITS ABSOLUTE BLACKNESS...!
SHE TELLS HERSELF NOT TO GIVE IN TO THE FEAR--
--A FEAR THAT IS BORN OF THE SECRET'S YOUNG CHILDHOOD.
CAPTURED AND CONFINED BY THE MYSTERIOUS DEO,* FOR YEARS HER ONLY HOME WAS A TINY AIRTIGHT CELL. HERE, HER STRANGE, ETHEREAL NATURE WAS STUDIED AND TESTED.
AND THOUGH SHE LONGED FOR ESCAPE AND THE PROMISE OF FREEDOM--
--HER CAPTORS WOULD DISCOVER NEW AND MORE HORRIBLE WAYS TO CONTAIN HER!
*DEPARTMENT OF EXTRAORDINARY OPERATIONS--Ed.
No. Can't--I don't have time for this now--have a job to do...
Everyone's counting...on me and Deadboy to capture Klarion...
But Deadboy's not very reliable right now... and I'm...the adult...the leader...
Have to rise above my fears...
I'm not gonna let this stop me!

THAT OUGHT TO HOLD HER!
Uh-oh...!
SSSKRAKT!
You'll have to do better than that, Klarion! I've been charged with bringing you in, and I plan to do just that!
OH, I HAVE PLENTY MORE WHERE THAT CAME FROM, GIRLFRIEND!--
--IF THAT DIDN'T HOLD YOU, HOW ABOUT--
How about THIS?!
uh...?
WITH THAT, SECRET 'SMOKE-JUMPS' THE WITCH BOY TO THE DARK AND HOPELESS PLACE SHE CALLS THE ABYSS-- THE 'DEFAULT' OF HER MYSTERIOUS TELEPORTATION--
POOOF!
HOWEVER...

POOOF
WHERE WAS THAT?! HELL? HADES? THE NETHER-WORLD?...
SORRY. BEEN THERE, DONE THAT, GOT THE T-SHIRT...
NOW LET'S TRY SOMETHING THAT'S REALLY FUN!
MEANWHILE...
MAN, THIS IS GREAT!! LISTEN TO THAT CROWD! IT'S LIKE I'M ALIVE AGAIN! IT'S LIKE--
POOOM
--LIKE I THINK I'M IN REALLY BIG TROUBLE!
CLAP! CLAP!
CLAP! CLAP!
YAY!
FUN
CLAP! CLAP!
YEA!
CLAP! CLAP!
ALL RIGHT!
CLAP! CLAP!
THERE IT IS, FOLKS! WHAT AN AMAZING CATCH!
YEAH!
tweet
JUST RELAX, PARTNER--I GOTCHA!!
WAY TO GO!!
CLAP! CLAP! CLAP! CLAP!
OOF!

UM, LOOK, I'M REALLY SORRY-- I JUST GOT, Y'KNOW, CARRIED AWAY... BY THE CIRCUS!
I GOT THE SAWDUST IN MY BLOOD, SEE?! IT'S IN MY HEART, IT'S IN MY SOUL! IT'S LIKE A DRUG, Y' HEAR ME?! GNAWIN' AT ME, GNAWIN' AT ME! EVERY TIME I THINK I'VE GOTTEN AWAY-- IT PULLS ME RIGHT BACK IN!! BUT IT WON'T HAPPEN AGAIN! I PROMISE YA! LEMME MAKE IT UP TO YA! YOU GOTTA GIMME ANOTHER CHANCE! PLEASEPLEASEPLEASE...!
Well...

LOOK AT THAT, TEEKL--THE WISPY-WITCH HAS A LITTLE DEAD FRIEND! OOO, I'M SCARED...!
'Kay--here's the plan. Their using Teekl as a decoy gave me an idea...
I'll do what I can to draw Klarion's attention while you try to sneak up behind him and...

I'M ON IT, BABY!
...baby?!
FOOSH
FOOSH!

Normally, it'd be easy for me to become completely intangible and let these blasts pass right through me--
--but we're talking magic here, and it seems that Klarion's got my number-- OUCH!
ZIMMM
ZIMM
ZZAT

OH, THIS IS GONNA BE GOOD! HE DOESN'T EVEN SEE IT COMING!

HA HA HA!
ZZAKT
UNGHH! I BEEN ZAPPED!

Deadboy, are you...
I THINK SO...
...BUT IT'S A GOOD THING I'M DEAD ALREADY...!

HAHA! GIVE UP, YOU WUSSES! YOU ARE NEVER GONNA BEAT ME!!--
--AFTER ALL, YER JUST A COUPLA KIDS, REALLY!!

THEN MAYBE IT'S TIME WE STARTED ACTING LIKE KIDS...?

WHAT ARE YOU GONNA DO NOW, BABIES? GONNA CRY...?

ACTUALLY, KLARION--IT GOES LIKE THIS...
...IT'S A LITTLE SOMETHING WE LEARNED THIS MORNING...
SEE... YOU'RE RIGHT! YOU'RE WINNING AND WE DON'T LIKE IT...

So instead of trying to beat you...
...WE'RE JUST GONNA TAKE YOUR THINGS!
SHPRAKT!
ROWR?!?
Eh? TEEKL?!?
WHOOOSH
Here, Kitty!
N-NO! YOU CAN'T! GIVE ME BACK MY--
AS EASY AS BREAKIN' A LITTLE KID'S SKATEBOARD...!
POOOF!
OH, BY THE WAY, KLARION-- B'BYE!
N-N-N-N--

NOOOOO!!!
GIMME BACK MY CAAAT!!
I'LL GET YOU TWO! I SWEAR IT! I'LL GET YOU!!

YEAH, WE KNOW IT ALL LOOKS REALLY CONFUSING. IT SEEMS LIKE MANY OF THE WORLD'S HEROES HAVE BEEN..."DE-AGED." NATURALLY, THIS WOULD PROMPT SOME CONCERN. HOWEVER...
...WE ASK THAT PEOPLE NOT PANIC. THINGS ARE NOT ALWAYS WHAT THEY SEEM. IN THIS DAY AND AGE, SEEING IS NO LONGER BELIEVING. REST ASSURED...
THAT THE TITANS HAVE EVERYTHING UNDER CONTROL.
WHERE'S THE CAMERA? BEAST BOY, YOU'RE IN MY LIGHT.
AN ABORTIVE ATTEMPT TO INTERVIEW THE SENIOR SPEEDSTER CALLING HIMSELF "IMPULSE" HAS LEFT A NUMBER OF QUESTIONS UP IN THE AIR. TO SAY NOTHING OF THE FACT...
...THAT YOUTHFUL "INCARNATIONS" OF SUCH KNOWN MENACES AS BLACK ADAM AND AMAZO HAVE BEEN REPORTED, LEAVING HAVOC IN THEIR WAKE. SO THE QUESTION STILL REMAINS...WHERE, AND IN WHAT CONDITION, ARE THE HEROES?
THAT LOIS LANE IS SOMETHING ELSE, ISN'T SHE.

THANKS AGAIN FOR THAT SPECIAL INSIGHT FROM LOIS LANE. MEANTIME, WASHINGTON LAW-MAKERS ARE STILL TRYING TO--
I DUNNO, I MEAN, ON THE ONE HAND, EVERYONE'S CRITICIZING THESE YOUNG HEROES. SAYING THEY SHOULDN'T BE OUT DOING THE STUFF THEY'RE DOING. BUT ME, I'M THINKING, ON THE OTHER HAND...

YOU'RE THINKING... AT LEAST THEY'RE DOING SOMETHING. WITH ALL THE GEN-X SLACKERS AND APATHY, IT'S IMPRESSIVE TO SEE YOUNG PEOPLE CARING ENOUGH TO PUT THEMSELVES ON THE LINE.
YEAH. YEAH, EXACTLY. I TELL YOU, KIDS ARE SO MUCH SMARTER NOWADAYS. ALL THIS COMPUTER STUFF... THEY JUST GET IT INSTANTLY.
PLUS, THEY HAVE ALL KINDS OF THINGS TO DEAL WITH THAT GUYS LIKE YOU... AND, UH, ME, NEVER HAD TO DEAL WITH.

DARNED STRAIGHT. NAME'S JACK, BY THE WAY.
I'M TIM.
REALLY? MY SON'S NAME IS TIM. YOU KIND OF REMIND ME OF HIM A LITTLE.
NO KIDDING. HE A GOOD KID?
THE BEST.
REALLY?

HEY, WHAT'RE YOU DRINKING?
OH, NOTHING FOR ME. LITTLE TAPPED OUT...

NONSENSE! HEY, FREDDY! GET MY PAL TIM, HERE, A BEER!
OH... NO, THAT'S OKAY. YOU DON'T HAVE TO--

TO KIDS!
TO KIDS!
KLINK

ACCCKKK!

OH, GEE, THANKS FOR SPRAYING ME WITH YOUR KOULBRAU.
WELL, I, UH... GUESS THIS BRAU WAS FOR YOU.
I'M LEAVING NOW.

SO... DID YOU ENJOY YOUR QUALITY TIME WITH YOUR FATHER?
I SMELL BEER ON YOUR BREATH.
I'D RATHER NOT DISCUSS IT.
AND THAT'S PRETTY MUCH AS FAR AS IT GOT.

ALL RIGHT... EVERYONE SHOULD BE BACK AT WHAT'S LEFT OF THE JUSTICE CAVE BY NOW.
LET'S HOPE THAT THERE'S BEEN SOME PROGRESS ON SOLVING THIS REVERSE AGING THING, BEFORE IT GETS COMPLETELY OUT OF CONTROL.

THE STUNNING CONCLUSION THAT WE HAD TO CALL:
Sins of Youth: The Stunning Conclusion
WILL SOMEONE TELL ME HOW TO DISCONNECT THE DARNED V-CHIP?
EXCUSE ME! PLASTIC MAN! DO WE HAVE TO HAVE ANOTHER WEDGIE DISCUSSION? DON'T MAKE ME COME OVER THERE!
PETER DAVID writer TODD NAUCK penciller
LARY STUCKER inker JASON WRIGHT colorist
KEN LOPEZ letterer MAUREEN McTIGUE associate editor
EDDIE BERGANZA editor

KIND OF REDEFINES "JUNIOR JUSTICE LEAGUE," DON'T'CHA THINK, MERRY?
OKAY, THAT'S IT! SOMEONE HERE IS HEADING FOR A HOSPITAL STAY!
DAN, YOU'RE ENJOYING THIS ENTIRELY TOO MUCH.
I GOTTA GO BAFFWOOM! WAAH!
NOW HOLD ON 'DERE! YA DON'T GOTTA RESORT TA' THREATS!
NOT THEM, DOIBY, ME! I'M GONNA CHECK IN AND GET MY TUBES TIED!

WILL YA GET DESE BRATS T'GEDDER SO'S I CAN LET 'EM HAVE IT WIT' DIS RAYGUN GIZMO AND MEBBE GET THIS WHOLE T'ING WRAPPED UP?!?
I HEARD HIM! IT'S JUST EASIER SAID THAN DONE! I MEAN, LOOK AT 'EM!
I'M STARTING TO THINK MAYBE THE WHOLE YOUNG HERO IDEA IS A LOUSY ONE!
STAR! DOIBY SAID TO--
NOW NOW, STAR, NO NEED TO MAKE A HASTY JUDGMENT.
OH, GREAT, I'M BEING LECTURED ON DECISION-MAKING BY IMPULSE! HEY... WHERE ARE WONDER WOMAN AND WONDER GIRL? AND SUPERMAN AND SUPERBOY!?

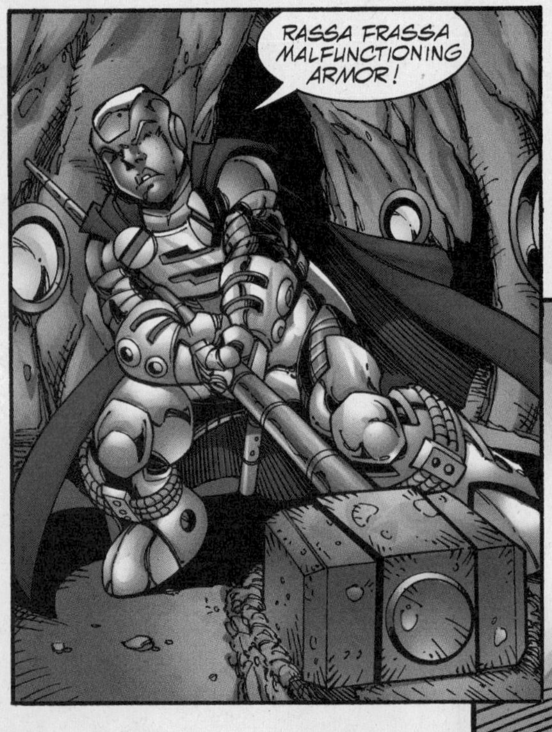

WOW! I LOOK BETTER THAN EVER!
YOU HAVEN'T CHANGED, YOU YUTZ!
I KNOW. BUT I WAS PRETTY KICKIN' TO BEGIN WITH!
DOIBY, WHAT'S WRONG WITH THE THING? AFTER THE TROUBLE YOU WENT THROUGH TO GET IT...
I DUNNO! IT SHOULD'A WOIKED POIFEKLY!
I CAN GUESS WHAT'S WRONG.
THE EFFECTS THAT BROUGHT ABOUT THIS CHANGE WERE A BLEND OF BOTH SCIENCE AND MAGIC. TWO DIFFERENT ENERGIES, AS IT WERE. WE CAN'T TRANSFORM BACK... UNLESS WE BLEND THOSE TWO PRECISE ENERGIES AGAIN. THE GUN ON ITS OWN WON'T WORK.
BATMAN'S RIGHT. WE NEED THE HELP OF THAT YOUNG SORCERER. THE ONE CALLED...
"KLARION THE WITCH BOY."
I KNOW YOU CREEPS WHO TOOK TEEKL ARE DOWN THERE! SHE'S MY FAMILIAR... MY ONLY FRIEND...
AND IF YOU THOUGHT THAT I, KLARION... BUM, BUM, BUM... THE WITCH BOY, MIGHT HAVE BEEN INSANE BEFORE... YOU AIN'T SEEN NOTHIN' YET!

DEADBOY! Are you still in Teekl's body?
NO, I WENT OUT FOR PIZZA AND A BREWSKI. OF COURSE I'M STILL--
POXY MONSTERS: THE NEXT WAVE
POXY MONSTERS: THE NEXT WAVE
DAWN GETS HITCHED
DEADLINE PRESSURE
POXY MONSTERS
POXY-MON$TERS
AVAILABLE EVERYWHERE!
ESBEE TOYS
WHOA, THAT POXY MONSTER STUFF IS CATCHING ON. MOVIES, GAMES...
I don't CARE about some children's pastime. I'm worried about whether you can maintain control of TEEKL if I take us BETWEEN.
BETWEEN WHAT?
Just... between. That'll get us away from KLARION and back to the--
UH oh.

PEEKABOOOO!!
The Spectral Annoyance
Poxy Monsters: The Next Wave
Big Fat Outline
Poxy Monsters: The Next Wave
Wednesday Matinee
Dawn Gets Hitched
Walking Parody
Deadline Pressure
PEEEEKABOOOOO!!!
WELL, AT LEAST IT'S NOT THE POWER RANGERS. THEY REALLY GOT ON MY NER--
Oh, SHUT UP!!!
HEH. MY LITTLE HORDES WILL BRING THEM DOWN QUICKLY ENOUGH. MEANTIME, MY JUNIOR INJUSTICE LEAGUE WILL BE KEEPING THE REST OF THE SUPERBRATS BUSY.

MEANWHILE...
YOUR ESCAPE IS NOTHING SHORT OF MIRACULOUS, MS. SPENCE.
IT'S GOOD TO HAVE YOU BACK HERE IN THE SAFETY OF OUR HEADQUARTERS.
MURDERER...! YOU KILLED TANA, YOU--
NOW, NOW... MURDERER IS SUCH AN UGLY WORD. I PREFER "MURDERESS."
NYARRRRHH!
HE'S LOOSE! THE SUPER-CLONE IS LOOSE!
WHAT TH--?!
A HOLOGRAM! YOU'RE A FREAKIN' HOLOGRAM!
FINE! I HAVE OTHER THINGS TO DO, THEN!

SMOOTH, KON. THE BIG, RESPONSIBLE GROWNUP. HERE I WAS TRYING TO BE A "TROJAN HORSE," WAITING TO PICK MY SPOT...
...AND THEN I SEE AMANDA SPENCE AND BLOW THE BIT. WELL, BETTER NOT MUFF THE ONE OPPORTUNITY I'VE GOT.
REPEATING, THIS IS SUPERMAN CALLING THE LEAGUE ON ALL FREQUENCIES. WE HAVE INFILTRATED THE AGENDA'S LAIR IN ALASKA. I'M SENDING THE LOCATION COORDINATES THROUGH NOW.
I THINK THEY'VE BEEN CALLING THE SHOTS ON THIS WHOLE THING... MANIPULATING EVERYONE, INCLUDING OLD JUSTICE! THEY ARE--

UH OH.
TAKE HIM DOWN, POINT MEN. HARD, FAST AND NASTY!

SO YOU REINED IN OUR YOUNG SUPERMAN. BRAVO... BUT NOT BEFORE HE WAS ABLE TO GET A MESSAGE OUT. WELL, WE'LL HAVE TO TAKE CERTAIN PRECAUTIONS. IF THERE IS NOTHING ELSE THEN...
THERE...IS, ACTUALLY. IN METROPOLIS, I THOUGHT I SAW SOMEONE WHO WAS...WELL... ME.
ME THE WAY I LOOKED BEFORE I WAS... CHANGED.
YOU AND YOUR FELLOW POINT MEN ARE CLONES... MANUFACTURED WITH THE MEMORIES AND PERSONALITIES OF THE INDIVIDUALS FROM WHOM YOU WERE CLONED.
THAT'S WHY WE'RE SO INTERESTED IN TRUE HEROES SUCH AS THE KRYPTONIAN.
YOU WERE ALWAYS SIMPLY A TEMPORARY MEASURE TO FILL THE SUPERHERO GAP. YOU'RE ROUGH DRAFTS...DISPOSABLE HEROES, AS IT WERE.
OH, BUT DON'T BE UPSET.
THERE ARE WORSE FATES THAN FINDING OUT YOU'RE NOT WHO YOU THINK YOU ARE.
YOU'D BE AMAZED HOW FEW FOLKS ARE.
BUT--
SO HARD TO GET GOOD HELP THESE DAYS. SPEAKING OF WHICH, I SHOULD REALLY CHECK IN ON KLARION...

NGH
STEEL...
ACKKK
AW, MAN! CAN'T YOU GUYS WEAR BELLS OR SOMETHING!
TORNADO, WHERE IS EVERYONE?
WILDBRAT SAID THEY WENT "BYE-BYE."
ACME CROWBAR
THERE WAS SOME KINDA EMERGENCY. WEIRD MONSTERS, PLUS KID SUPERVILLAINS, TEARING APART GOTHAM AND METROPOLIS AND HAPPY HARBOR.
OH, PERFECT.
WEIRD TRANSFORMATIONS... MOB SCENES OF HEROES...EVERYTHING COMING UNGLUED...
WHY DOES STUFF LIKE THIS SEEM TO HAPPEN EVERY FIFTH WEEK OR SO?

AND SO THE "APPROXIMATELY" FIFTH WEEK CHAOS CONTINUES, AS THE "JUNIOR INJUSTICE LEAGUE" OF KLARION RAMPAGES THROUGH THE TARGETED TOWNS...
...PROVING MORE THAN A MATCH FOR THE FAR MORE NUMEROUS, BUT FAR LESS FOCUSED, KID HEROES.
AS KLARION OVERSEES IT ALL, OLD HOSTILITIES, FUELED BY YOUNG HORMONES, SEND THE CHAOS LEVEL THROUGH THE ROOF EVERYWHERE. EVERYWHERE, THAT IS, EXCEPT ONE PLACE...
SAM AND JANET EVENING! BWAAAHAHAHAAAA! SPHINX, THAT'S GREAT!
HERE'S ANOTHER. "KNOCK KNOCK..."

FAIR PLAY

I HAVEN'T HAD SO MUCH FUN SINCE I GAVE JIM JONES MY KOOL-AID RECIPE.
HELLO, KLARION.
CONTESSA! YOUR HOLOTECH IS MORE SOPHISTICATED THAN I WOULD HAVE THOUGHT.
I'M GLAD YOU APPROVE.
I HAVE NEED OF YOU.
AND I HAVE NEED OF TEEKL! WITHOUT HER, IT'S BECOMING MORE AND MORE DIFFICULT TO CONCENTRATE MY EFFORTS. BUT SECRET AND THAT GHOST ARE ELUDING ME!
ME, KLARION... BUM, BUM, BUM... THE WITCH BOY!
MY HEART BLEEDS WE'VE OTHER PROBLEMS.
YOU HAVE OTHER PROBLEMS, NOT ME.
I DON'T HAVE TIME FOR THIS.
WHAT IN SEVEN HELLS?! HOW DID--?
NOW LISTEN CAREFULLY, KLARION. OUR ALASKA HEADQUARTERS MAY BE COMING UNDER ATTACK.
I WANT YOU TO MARSHAL YOUR FORCES TO DEFEND IT. WE HAVE WHAT WE WANT, AND NOW IT'S TIME TO ANNIHILATE THE REST OF THE HEROES.
BUT TEEKL IS--
KLARION... PICK UP YOUR TOYS AND PUT THEM WHERE I SAY... OR I WILL SEND YOU TO YOUR ROOM... PERMANENTLY.
VERY WELL...
STRANGELY QUIESCENT, KLARION DOES AS ORDERED... AND AT ALL THE SITES OF BATTLE, THE YOUNG VILLAINS AND POXY MONSTER GROUNDTROOPS VANISH.

WHILE, AT THE MOMENT, IN A PLACE THAT IS NO PLACE...
MEEERAWRRR!!
SECRET! SHOOK ME LOOSE! SECRET, DID YOU HEAR--?!?
I heard.
Little creature... you think to ESCAPE ME in this place?
I AM THIS PLACE!
MRAWRR--
--RRRR-!-
HUNH. SO THAT WAS "BETWEEN." NOT EXACTLY WHERE I'D WANNA BUILD MY SUMMER HOME.
WH'HAPPENED TO TEEKL?
Curiosity and her type don't MIX well.

WOW. LOOK AT HER: A POWER FAMILIAR FOR A SORCERER, AND EVEN SHE WAS THROWN BY SPENDING TIME IN YOU.
And you're NOT?
EH. DEAD GUYS DON'T SHOCK EASY. SO...DO YOU THINK THE OTHERS WILL BE BACK ANYTIME--
THUMPA THUMPA THUMPA
--SOON.
THEY STILL ALL LOOK RIDICULOUS.
They appear to have FLATTENED Teekl. What should we DO?
LET'S GO BUM MONEY. AFTER ALL, NO ONE CAN RESIST A PRETTY GIRL WITH A SAD PUSS.
HERE. THIS IS YOURS.
SWELL. THANKS A LOT.
WUH... UH--
OOOHH NUTS!!

...MANIPULATING EVERYONE, INCLUDING OLD JUSTICE! THEY ARE--
THE AGENDA. I KNEW THIS THING WAS SMELLING MORE AND MORE WRONG.
YOU'VE GOT TO GO TO WASHINGTON. TELL PERKINS...
TELL HIM WHAT? THAT EVERYTHING WE SAID WAS WRONG? IT WASN'T WRONG.
WE MADE VALID POINTS. YES, IT WAS TURNED INTO A MEDIA CIRCUS.
BUT LOOK AT THESE HEROES AS KIDS!
THEY'RE HEROES AS KIDS... BUT WE WERE KIDS AS HEROES.
DID WE "TURN OUT" THAT BADLY?
NO. PRETTY DARNED WELL, ACTUALLY. DAN...
SIGH OKAY...I GET THE IDEA. CYCLONE TWINS, WITH ME!
CYCLONE TWIN POWERS, ACTIVATE!
POWER OF... WATER!
SHAPE OF... A PAIL!
HEY! "AQUABABY" JUST KICKED THE BUCKET!
WHOA! DÉJÀ VU!
LET'S GET GOING BEFORE THE JOKES GET WORSE.
THEY COULDN'T POSSIBLY.
REDDY, THERE'S SOMETHING I'D LIKE YOU TO ATTEND TO.
HOKAY, ROBIN. YOU'RE THE BOSS.
YEAH... YEAH, I GUESS I AM.

YOUR PLAN WORKED ALL TOO WELL, MS. SPENCE. WE GOT SOME INSIGHT INTO JUST HOW POWERFUL HIS TACTILE TELEKINESIS POWER HAS BECOME. THE READINGS WENT OFF THE CHART.
WHERE'S WONDER... GIRL?! I INSIST YOU BRING HER HERE IMMEDIATELY!
SHE'S ON HER WAY BACK; THE TESTS ARE COMPLETED ON HER.
HER POWERS ARE MOST CURIOUS. THEY DON'T SEEM TO DEVELOP FROM ANY GENE OR TRAINING OR PHYSIOLOGY.
IT'S ALMOST AS IF THEY WERE "CONFERRED" ON HER MAGICALLY. VERY CURIOUS.
WELL, WELL! LOOK WHO'S HERE!
MOVE, PLEASE.
AND IF WE DON'T WANNA?

WHAT'S THE DELAY HERE? PEOPLE, OUT OF THE WAY!
BUT WE'RE NOT "PEOPLE," ARE WE, MS. SPENCE?
WE'RE... THINGS. GHOSTS WITH DELUSIONS OF LIFE. CREATIONS. CLONES.
SO YOU FOUND OUT. VERY WELL... YES. THAT'S TRUE ENOUGH.
YOU'D DO WELL TO REMEMBER THAT, AND OBEY.
"REMEMBER THAT"? YER KIDDIN', RIGHT? I MEAN, LIKE, WE'RE GONNA FORGET THAT?
SHE'S FULL OF IT! WHATEVER YOUR ORIGINS, YOU CAN THINK AND FEEL! YOU CAN DO AS YOU DESIRE! WHERE YOU COME FROM ISN'T AS IMPORTANT AS WHERE YOU'RE GOING!
AND WE KNOW WHERE YOU'RE GOING, "WONDER WOMAN."
WENDY... JOEY... STEP ASIDE. NOW.
DO AS SHE SAYS, JOEY.
VERY WISE.
HEY! GUYS! SOME OF MY BEST FRIENDS ARE CLONES!

ALASKA...
HEY, ADAM! LOOK OVER HERE!
SO HELP ME, COLD, YOU PITCH ONE MORE SNOWBALL AT ME, I'LL SHOVE A BAG OF ICE UP YOUR--
QUIET, ALL OF YOU! I THINK I SEE SOMETHING OUT TH--
OH, NO!
KLARION, WHAT'S WRONG?
TEEKL! WHAT HAVE THEY DONE TO HER!
TEEEEKLLLLL!
Stop right there.
Transform them back, Klarion. Combine your powers with Mr. Dickles's weapon here...
...or I'll KILL her.
YOU DON'T DICTATE TO ME!
I can feel your powers WANING as your desperation increases.
It takes all your strength just to maintain the current output.

SURRENDER, Klarion. This is your LAST CHANCE...and hers.

UHM... IS SHE BLUFFING?
IT'S A SECRET.

ALL RIGHT. I CAN'T... I DON'T WANT...TO LIVE WITHOUT HER. JUST... DON'T HURT HER AND I'LL DO WHATEVER YOU SAY.

WHAT?!?
SHUT UP! NONE OF YOU MATTER! ONLY TEEKL MATTERS!
ZZZWAK
OOOFFF!
WHAT IN ALL THE COVENS--?

GREETINGS, KLARION. YOU'RE A LOT SMALLER THAN I REMEMBER.
WELL, DIS CAN'T BE GOOD.
WHAT SORT OF FOUL MAGIC IS THIS?
NOT MAGIC. SCIENCE. INDISTINGUISHABLE AT TIMES, I ADMIT.
WE WASTE NOTHING AT THE AGENDA, KLARION. THE TEACUP YOU HELD WHEN WE DINED TOGETHER WAS A DNA SCANNER.
AND SINCE YOU'RE A BEING OF MAGIC... WE COULD GROW THE CLONE OF YOU IN NO TIME. YOU HELP REDEFINE THE RULES. SAY HELLO TO KLARION...
...BUM BUM BUM... THE WITCH MAN!
ONE WHO HAS NO USE FOR PRETENTIOUS KITTENS...OR YOUNGER, UNFORTUNATE INCARNATIONS. AND NOW--

--LET'S HAVE A FIGHT SCENE!!!
IT WILL BE A SHORT ONE AFTER I GET THROUGH WITH YOU!
OOO. SCARE ME, LITTLE MAN.
THIS GIG IS GONNA GET ME TO NETWORK!
WELL? DID I PROMISE YOU THE STORY OF A LIFETIME, ACE?

MEANWHILE, INSIDE...
EXCUSE ME, SHORTCUT... WHAT ARE YOU DOING HE--?
GROUNDSWELL, NOW!
I'M ON IT, SHORTCUT.
WE'RE CLEAR! THAT OVERSIZED DIRT PILE DISRUPTED THE POWER SUPPLY AND SET US FREE!
IT'S TOO EASY! WHY ARE THEY HELPING US?
IT'S A LONG STORY. GO READ THE MINISERIES. COME ON!
MINISERIES?
DON'T LOOK AT ME.

OKAY, GENTLEMEN: LET'S STAY FOCUSED!
CHECK THE BABE IN THE MINISKIRT! TOTALLY HOT!
WAY TO FOCUS THERE, "KID FLESH."
"KID FLESH!" GOOD ONE, IMPULSE.
WAY TO SUCK UP, SAUCER HEAD.
AWWW, BITE ME!
SOMEBODY STOP AMAZO! HE'S GOING FOR MERRY!
WE'RE ON IT! LET 'ER RIP, PLAS!
AW, BARNACLES! GREAT AIM, RUBBER BOY!
ARRHHH!
ZAKOOOM
NICE ONE, STAR.
BACK AT'CHA.

DEADBOY--! I need YOU to--
WAY AHEAD OF YOU, SMOKY.
C'MON, KITTY... TIME FOR YOU TO GO BACK TO YOUR MASTER!
WHOA. I'VE GOT THIS SUDDEN URGE TO COUGH UP A HAIRBALL.
THINK I'LL DO IT ON PENGUIN'S SHOES.
IMPRESSIVE THAT EVEN AS TEENS, YOU'RE CAUSING AGGRAVATION.
LET'S SEE IF DOWNGRADING YOU TO INFANCY WILL KEEP YOU IN LINE.
AH... TEEKL. MUSTN'T LET YOU INTERFERE.
TIME TO TEAR YOUR KIBBLES TO BITS.

OOOOFF!
SO, WE MEET AGAIN... SORT OF...
TEEKL! IT'S YOU!
AND YOU...
YOU'RE A BAD MAN.
YOU'RE A VERY BAD MAN.
GET HIM!
ARRHHHHH!!!

WHILE, INSIDE AGENDA HEADQUARTERS...

KEEP ON 'EM! WE'VE GOT 'EM ON THE RUN!

HEADS UP! SECOND WAVE COMING IN, THROUGH THE SOUTH ENTRANCE!

HELLO, MANDY! READY TO DIE?
SUPERBOY!
I'M GLAD YOU MANAGED TO GET AWAY FROM YOUR CAPTORS AND WIND UP HERE. BECAUSE NOW I GET TO DO TO YOU WHAT YOU DID TO TANA!
KON! NO!
STAY OUTTA THIS, WONDY! THIS ENDS HERE!
WRONG! YOU KILL HER AND IT STARTS HERE! OR HAVE YOU FORGOTTEN...
...WHEN YOU WERE THERE FOR... ARROWETTE? SHE WALKED AWAY FROM US, FROM HER IDENTITY... HER NAME. ARE YOU GOING TO GIVE UP WHAT YOUR NAME STANDS FOR?
WELL?
HEH.

EEEYAAHHHH!!!
"HEH" THIS, WITCH!
NOOOO!

OKAY, HE'S DOWN! NOW WE JUST HAVE TO FIGURE OUT A WAY TO HOLD HIM UNTIL--
NO. WE DON'T.
EEYIIIII
I WILL NOT SUFFER THAT WITCH TO LIVE. AND AS FOR THE REST OF YOU...
OH, DEVIL TAKE IT. I'M TIRED OF THIS GAME. OF BEING LIED TO AND USED. I'M GOING TO GO FIND ANOTHER GAME.
PEEKABOOOOOO?!

You said you would restore EVERYONE to their NATURAL state!
YOU PRESSURED ME INTO IT. PROMISES UNDER DURESS HAVE NO--
MRROOWWRRRR
OH, ALL RIGHT, TEEKL, IF YOU INSIST.
BUT "EVERYONE" IT IS...OR NO ONE.
--LOSE TRANSMISSION ANY SECOND! AND--THEY'VE CAPTURED! MS. SPENCE! AND--
SHE'S ALIVE. INTERESTING. I WOULD HAVE THOUGHT HE'D HAVE KILLED HER AFTER THE DEMISE OF HIS LITTLE GIRLFRIEND. WELL... NO MATTER.
BUT OUR HEADQUAR
AS IF THAT WAS THE AGENDA'S ONLY PLACE OF BUSINESS. IT WAS WORTH SACRIFICING IT TO OBTAIN KRYPTONIAN DNA...AND AMAZONIAN DNA AS WELL.
IN THE END, THE REST IS JUST NOISE AND STORM.

SUZIE, WHAT DO YOU MEAN, YOU DON'T WANT TO GO BACK TO BEING A TEEN?! YOU'VE... YOU'VE GOT TO!
I don't "got to" do ANYTHING, Cassie. NO ONE tells me what to do, EVER!
I'm DONE hiding. I don't EVER want to go back to that childlike feeling of helplessness, of people hurting me... EVER.
IF SHE WON'T CHANGE BACK, IT'S NOT "EVERYONE," AND I'M OFF THE HOOK. TIME IS TICKING.
I don't understand how YOU can want to go back to being a teen, Kon. You've finally got what you've wanted...
EXCEPT I WANT THE SUPERBOY NAME TO MEAN SOMETHING... AS MUCH AS THE SUPERMAN NAME DOES. SOMEBODY REMINDED ME OF THAT... RIGHT, WONDY?
I WOULD HAVE GOTTEN AWAY WITH IT IF IT WEREN'T FOR THOSE BLASTED GROWNUPS!
SECRET... NOT WANTING TO BE HURT... THAT NEVER GOES AWAY, WHETHER YOU'RE AN ADULT OR A TEEN.
BUT "HURT" CAN BE HANDLED... IF YOU'VE GOT FRIENDS WHO ARE GOING TO STICK WITH YOU.
BE THERE FOR YOU, AS WE WILL BE.

And you promise YOU'LL be there for me, Robin... ALWAYS?
ABSOLUTELY.
I'VE GOT A BAD FEELING ABOUT THAT PROMISE.
ME TOO.
OKAY, WITCHY BOY... LET 'ER RIP!
YAWN IF YOU INSIST.
THEY DID IT!
WE'RE BACK TO NORMAL!
Whoopee.

KON! YOU LOOK TERRIFIC! AND THIS IS AS GOOD A TIME AS ANY TO TELL YOU--
PAIN?
NO, I'M NOT IN PAIN, I'M IN--
WAIT... PAIN?
YOU ALMOST BROKE ME IN HALF! MY... MY POWERS... WHAT'S HAPPENED TO--?
NOT MY PROBLEM! I'VE KEPT MY WORD.
EVERYONE ON EARTH HAS BEEN RESTORED TO THEIR REGULAR SELVES. TA.
"ON EARTH." ODD PHRASING.
IS THIS THE PART WITH THE MORAL? 'CAUSE I ALWAYS LOVE THIS PAR--
ACTUALLY, ACE. I'M REMINDED OF THE LATIN PROVERB, QUAE PECCAMUS JUVENES EA LUMINUS SENES. THE SINS OF YOUTH ARE PAID FOR IN OLD AGE.
MEANING?
THAT YOUTH CAN BE GUIDED BY THE OLD, AND THE OLD BY THE YOUNG.
MERRY! WONDER GIRL! WHAT CAN WE TAKE AWAY FROM ALL THIS?
THAT YOUNG PEOPLE NEED PROTECTION? THAT OLD PEOPLE ARE OUT OF TOUCH? THAT--
AND THAT EVERYONE, NO MATTER WHAT AGE, HAS A LOT TO LEARN.

SOME MORE THAN OTHERS.
SIGH TELL ME ABOUT IT.
GRAN'PA... YOU THINK THAT'S TRUE?
TELL ME WHAT YOU THINK.
VROOM
I'LL TELL YOU WHAT I THINK!
I THINK WHEN I FIND THE MAGIC-TOSSIN' BASTICH WHO TURNED THE MAIN MAN INTO THE TOP TOT...
I'M GONNA FRAG 'IM, THAT'S WHAT!
THE END?

cover gallery

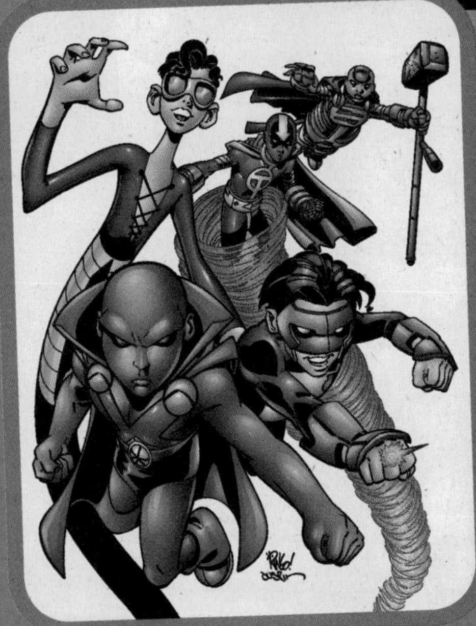